POWER TALKS
TALKS
BULLSH*T
WALKS

HOW TO DOMINATE YOUR WORKPLACE WHEN THE SYSTEM IS RIGGED AGAINST YOU

MARY ROBBINS

ISBN: 979-8-9985361-1-3

For inquiries, permission requests, or bulk orders contact the publisher at info@threebrospublishing.com

DEDICATUM
FORTIBUS FEMINIS

— To Strong Women

CONTENTS

PART 2: The Network Effect

PART 3: Personas & Personalities

INTRODUCTION

Your Power Has Been Waiting for You

Hey there.

If you're reading this right now, or maybe listening while you're driving, you're about to learn secrets that will change how you think about everything.

This isn't just another book that's going to sit on your shelf. This is your wake-up call. Your opportunity to finally understand what's really happening around you.

I see you. I see how hard you've been working. How you show up every day, giving your best, wondering why it sometimes feels like you're speaking a different language than everyone else in the room. Wondering why your ideas get overlooked. Why that promotion went to someone else. Why you feel like you're always playing catch-up in a game where nobody told you the rules.

It's not you. It's not that you're not smart enough, not worthy enough, not ready enough. The truth is, there's been a whole conversation about power happening around you. And nobody invited you to join it.

Until now.

Learning the Hard Way

My name is Mary Robbins, and I learned these lessons the hardest way possible. By living through every single mistake first.

I didn't come from the perfect home with a father figure who taught me the unwritten rules of success. I left home at 18 and had to figure out everything on my own. No safety net. No insider knowledge. Just grit and survival instinct.

As the stepdaughter and oldest sibling, I got the basics. Keep your room clean, watch your siblings, make good grades, stay out of trouble. There was structure, discipline, and expectation, but not much guidance about how to speak up for myself, challenge ideas in a room, or navigate ambition with confidence.

My stepfather had a dated, conservative view that women belonged at home. He never taught me how to ask for a raise or challenge ideas in meetings or protect my time. Those were things I later realized other people learned from their fathers. After leaving home, I found myself nearly starving on cold London streets, walking in shoes with gaping holes in the soles, wearing clothes more suitable for spring than winter.

I eventually got on the right track, but the workplace lessons came through brutal experience. I learned the hard way when I stayed quiet and watched my ideas get repeated by louder voices. When I was told to smile more. When I was intimidated by a male coworker who threatened me not to invade his "space" and followed it up by literally trying to run my car off the road.

It all seemed like a hill too hard to climb. I just didn't have the tools or understanding of the politics within the workplace. Certainly not the depth of the dynamics at play.

It wasn't until I read Robert Greene's "The 48 Laws of Power" that everything clicked. His work breaks down the manipulation tactics powerful men have used throughout history. These narcissistic tactics get weaponized against women at work all the time. They're designed to maintain male power. Period. Here's what hit me: nobody teaches women these power games. We're expected to navigate them blind.

But understanding the game didn't stop me from getting crushed by it.

When the stress finally broke me one evening and I found myself crying, exhausted from trying to do everything perfectly and invisibly, my husband said something that changed everything. "If this were happening to me, I'd be handling it differently. Not because I'm smarter. Because I was taught to."

He was right.

What We're Going to Do Together

What we're going to explore together isn't the cold, calculating kind of power you've probably seen before. You know what I'm talking about. The manipulation, the ego trips, the way some people climb ladders by stepping on others. That's not us. That's never going to be us.

But just because we don't want to be ruthless doesn't mean we have to be powerless.

This book is everything I wish I'd had during those brutal early years. It's not theory. It's tested, hard-earned, field-ready guidance. Every page is designed to give you tools that are immediately accessible, easy to understand, and ready to act on.

If your father didn't teach you these things, that's okay. I will.

Last week, I met a brilliant marketing analyst in line at Starbucks as I was waiting on my caffeine fix. She told me about her job and confided her frustration. "I keep getting passed over," she said. "I do great work, but somehow I'm invisible." As we talked, it became clear she knew how to do the work, but she didn't know how to navigate the unspoken dynamics that actually determine who gets ahead.

Sound familiar?

You're not alone in this. Every woman I've ever worked with has felt this way at some point. We've all had those moments where we realize we've been playing by one set of rules while everyone else is playing by another. Those moments sting. They make us question ourselves. But they're also wake-up calls.

And your wake-up call led you here.

So this journey is about seeing clearly. It's about understanding the patterns that have been there all along. It's about finally having the tools to respond instead of just react.

Think about the last time someone took credit for your idea. Remember how that felt? That confusion mixed with frustration? That moment when you wondered if you were imagining things? That's what happens when we can't see the power dynamics at play. We blame ourselves instead of recognizing the move that was made against us.

But what if I told you that once you start seeing these patterns, everything changes? What if you could walk into any room and immediately understand what's really happening? What if you could protect your ideas, build your influence, and advance your career without compromising who you are?

That's exactly what we're going to do together.

This book isn't going to be like those corporate leadership manuals that make you feel like you need to become a different person to succeed. You know the ones. They're written by people who've never had to navigate being the only woman in the room, who've never had their tone policed or their ambition questioned.

This is different. This is written by someone who gets it. Who's been there. Who's made the mistakes and learned the lessons and now wants to save you some of the heartache.

Every chapter we dive into together is going to feel like sitting down with your smartest friend over coffee. I'm going to share stories from my life, from the incredible women I've had the privilege to work with, and from leaders you probably know. We're going to laugh a little, maybe get fired up a little, and definitely have some moments that make everything click into place.

You don't have to choose between being kind and being powerful. You don't have to choose between collaboration and advancement. You don't have to choose between being yourself and influence.

You can have it all. And I'm going to show you how.

But first, when was the last time you really looked around your workplace and saw it clearly? Not through the lens of how things should be, but how they actually are? Who has the real influence? Who gets their way without making a fuss? Who seems to have information that others don't?

These observations aren't gossip. They're intelligence. And intelligence is power.

I remember when this first clicked for me. I was sitting in a leadership meeting, watching one of my colleagues consistently interrupt the women in the room. But only when our boss was present. When it was just our team, he was perfectly respectful. That's when I realized this wasn't about him being rude. This was strategic. He was positioning himself as the dominant voice in front of the person who mattered most.

Once I saw that pattern, I couldn't unsee it. And once I couldn't unsee it, I could start responding differently.

That's what this book is going to do for you. It's going to turn on a light you didn't even know was there.

Each chapter starts with a principle. Think of these as universal truths about how power actually works. But then we translate that principle into language that works for us. Into strategies that honor who we are.

I'll switch up how I explain things because our conversation should feel natural, not scripted. This isn't a lecture. This is a mentoring session.

And throughout our time together, I'm going to ask you to pause. To reflect. To look around. These aren't just random questions. They're designed to keep you present, to help you see your own situation more clearly. Because awareness is the first step to transformation.

I also want to acknowledge something that might be hard to hear. Sometimes, we accidentally make ourselves easy targets. Maybe we overshare with the wrong person. Maybe we dim our light to make others comfortable. Maybe we wait for permission instead of taking initiative.

This doesn't make you weak or naive. It makes you human. And more importantly, it makes you teachable. The women who grow the most are the ones willing to look honestly at their own patterns.

Here's what I promise you'll gain from our time together.

First, you'll develop radar. You'll sense power moves the moment they happen, sometimes before the person making them even realizes what they're doing.

Second, you'll have a toolkit. Real strategies, specific language, concrete actions you can take starting tomorrow.

And third, you'll build presence. The kind of quiet confidence that comes from knowing you can handle whatever comes your way.

This book will walk you through the moves, the mindset, and the strategies that no one hands to women early enough. You'll get familiar with the power plays, the unwritten rules, and the office politics that shape careers behind closed doors. The goal isn't just survival. It's influence, confidence, and control.

Before we dive into our first principle together, try this. Think of one situation recently where you felt confused or frustrated by someone's behavior at work. Hold that situation in your mind as we go through these chapters. I guarantee you'll start seeing exactly what was really happening. And more importantly, how you can handle it differently next time.

The fact that you're here, reading this, tells me everything I need to know about you. You're ready. You're brave enough to look at power honestly. You're willing to learn a new way of navigating your professional world.

And that combination of readiness and courage? That's going to change everything for you.

You're not behind. You're about to get ahead.

So take a deep breath. Get comfortable. Maybe grab that cup of tea or coffee.

It's time to claim what's been yours all along.

WHAT IS POWER?

It sounds like a straightforward question, but the answer is everything.

Power is your ability to make things happen. It means having a say in decisions, getting access to what you need, shaping the world around you, and steering outcomes.

At work, it's about getting a seat at the table when big decisions are made, having people actually listen when you speak up, getting the opportunities that move your career forward, and having the authority to help others or call out BS when you see it.

Here's the thing about power for women in the workplace: it's complicated. You can see it, but it feels just out of reach. Companies talk about it and even promise it, but they do not always deliver. It shows up in everyday moments. You see it in who gets listened to in meetings and who gets credit for ideas. You also see it in who gets tapped for leadership roles and who gets noticed instead of ignored. It's there in how much you get paid, whether you get promoted, and all those unwritten rules about "how things work around here."

But here's what I want you to know: power isn't just about your job title or corner office. It's also in what you know that nobody can take away from you. It's in the connections you build with people who genuinely have your back. It's in finding the guts to speak up for yourself and other women. And it's in the magic that happens when women support each other instead of competing.

Real empowerment means figuring out how power works. It includes the obvious stuff and the sneaky stuff, then going after it intentionally. It means calling out the old systems that keep power in the same hands and creating new ones where talent matters more than tradition.

Over the next 48 "Power Talks," we're breaking down exactly how to build real power at work. We're going to deep dive on how to expand your influence in rooms that matter, defend yourself against the BS, and go on the offensive to create opportunities for yourself and the women around you. Plus, we're getting into how to build your power circle networks, the people who will open doors for you, and decode the different personas you'll deal with so you can navigate office dynamics like a pro.

(If you want to dig deeper on the mechanics and the "how-to" of any power principle, check out my first book, The 48 Laws of Power for Women Fed Up with Male Workplace Dominance. I've got you covered with the full breakdown including how to defend yourself against powerplays.)

Part I

48 Power Talks

♀

RADIATE CONFIDENCE
NOT COMPETITION

You know that feeling when you're absolutely killing it at work, and suddenly your boss gets weird? Distant? Critical of everything you do?

That's their insecurity talking, not your performance.

This is the first thing you need to understand about navigating professional power: when someone feels threatened by your competence, they start closing doors instead of opening them.

So let me be clear about what we're doing here. Nobody's asking you to shrink yourself or dim your light. We're talking about being strategic with your brilliance so you can keep rising without accidentally making yourself a target.

One of my biggest early mistakes involved a VP who needed to be the star of every meeting. The center of attention, the source of all good ideas. And I kept presenting my ideas as mine. "Here's my plan." "My research shows." "I think we should..."

Every single time, he tore my ideas apart. Not because they were bad, but because his ego couldn't handle someone else being brilliant in his vicinity.

So I got smarter. I started saying things like, "This builds on that direction you set last quarter. Here's how we can take it even further." Same ideas. Different packaging.

He started championing my work. My name was still attached to the results, but he felt like the mentor who'd guided me there.

That's what I mean by directing your shine. You're not getting smaller. You're getting smarter.

Look at Indra Nooyi when she was transforming PepsiCo. She didn't storm into boardrooms demanding credit or competing with the CEO. She positioned herself as the strategic partner who made his vision better. And she became one of the most powerful CEOs in the world.

Her brilliance was undeniable, but she never made the people above her feel threatened by it.

There's a huge difference between strategic framing and letting someone steal your work. If someone takes credit for your idea completely, you address it. Just not in a way that makes you look petty or them look threatened.

A friend of mine watched her manager present her entire project plan as his own. She was furious. Instead of calling him out in front of everyone, she waited until the next leadership meeting and said, "I'm glad the strategy I developed is getting traction. Here's the data that supports it."

No drama. No accusations. Just a gentle reminder of where the brilliance originated.

Sometimes we make ourselves the target. When you correct your boss in front of the whole team. When you turn every meeting into your personal TED talk. When you announce every win like you're accepting an Oscar.

You're not being confident. You're being careless.

This doesn't mean you should dim yourself. It means you need to read the room. Pick your moments. Save your boldest moves for when they'll have the biggest impact.

Think of it as "don't poke the bear while you're still in its cave."

Here's what you need to do: Grab a notebook and do an honest inventory. Write down one area where you've been playing too small, where you're hiding your light when you should be letting it shine. Then write down one area where you might be pushing your brilliance in ways that are creating unnecessary friction.

For the first area, plan one concrete step to move forward more boldly. For the second? Adjust your framing. Tie your work to shared goals. Give others some credit. Let someone else have the spotlight for a minute before you step back into it.

The goal isn't to make yourself small. It's to stay in the room, build real influence, and shine in ways that last.

Men often use this principle to undercut and dominate. We use it to collaborate, elevate, and protect our long-term credibility.

You don't need to diminish yourself for anyone. But you do need to be smart about when you step forward and when you create space for others.

When you shine with intention and strategy, you rise without having to apologize for taking up space.

BUILD CIRCLES THAT LIFT, NOT CAGES THAT LIMIT

So I need to tell you about the most painful lesson I learned in my twenties, and I'm still kind of angry about it.

I had this colleague, Maya. We grabbed lunch together constantly, chatted often after hours, bonded over impossible deadlines and difficult clients. She felt like my work sister. My safe person in that office.

One day I'm frustrated with our director's leadership style. Really frustrated. The kind of frustrated where you need to vent to someone or you're going to explode in a meeting.

So I vent to Maya. I tell her my honest concerns about the team's direction. I tell her I'm considering looking for other opportunities. I trust her completely.

Two weeks later, I'm in a meeting with that same director, and the energy is completely different. Cold. Suspicious. She's questioning my commitment to the team. My attitude. Whether I'm "really invested in our success."

I had no idea what was happening.

Then after the meeting, someone pulls me aside. "You know Maya went to her, right? Told her everything you said. Framed it like she was 'concerned about your attitude.'"

I felt like I'd been punched in the stomach.

Maya got promoted six months later.

That's when I understood something fundamental about workplace relationships. They operate under different rules than personal friendships. The stakes are higher. The loyalty is thinner. And envy can turn affection into sabotage faster than you'd ever imagine.

I'm not telling you to become cold and distant at work. Human connection matters. Support systems matter. But you need to be strategic about what you share and who you trust with career-defining information.

Work friends can be wonderful. But work friends with competing ambitions? That's where things get complicated.

If your work friend got offered your dream job, would they turn it down out of loyalty to you? Probably not. And you wouldn't expect them to. That's the reality of professional life.

But here's what's interesting about this story. Remember how I said Maya felt like my safe person?

I had another colleague, David, who drove me absolutely crazy. Every project I pitched, he had questions. Every strategy I suggested, he had concerns. I thought he was just being difficult.

But his constant pushback made me sharper. I started anticipating objections before presenting ideas. I built stronger cases. I thought through blind spots I would have missed.

When I finally presented to senior leadership, I was bulletproof. Because David had already hit me with every possible criticism.

He wasn't my friend. He was my critic. But he made me better.

Maya was my friend. And she torpedoed my career for a promotion.

So which relationship was actually more valuable?

I think about this a lot now. How we're conditioned to trust the people who make us feel good and avoid the people who challenge us. But sometimes that's exactly backwards.

The person who tells you what you want to hear might be protecting themselves, not you. The person who pushes back on your ideas might be the one actually helping you succeed.

I'm not saying David was doing it out of kindness. He probably just liked being right. But the effect was the same.

These days, I set clear boundaries around what I share at work. Personal frustrations about leadership? I keep those to myself or share them outside work entirely. Career anxieties? I talk to mentors outside my company. Complaints about colleagues? Absolutely not.

And when it comes to critics? I engage them strategically. I find out what they actually care about. Sometimes the person who challenges you most can become your strongest ally once you understand their perspective.

A few months after the Maya disaster, I started inviting David to weigh in on my proposals before I presented them. Turned out his background was in risk assessment, and his concerns usually flagged things I'd overlooked.

We never became friends. But we developed a professional respect that actually moved my career forward.

Maya? I haven't spoken to her in five years. She probably thinks I'm holding a grudge.

I'm not. I'm just done trusting people who've proven they'll throw me under the bus for their own advancement.

The lesson isn't that everyone's out to get you. It's that workplace loyalty is transactional, not automatic. And the sooner you understand that, the better you can protect yourself while still building genuine connections with people who've actually earned your trust.

Not every friend is safe, and not every critic is a threat.

That's the truth Maya taught me. Expensive lesson. But I'm glad I learned it when I did.

3

DON'T SHOW YOUR
HAND TOO SOON

I need to tell you about something I did that still makes me cringe when I think about it.

I had this incredible project idea. One that could revolutionize how my entire team handled our biggest challenge. I was practically bursting with excitement about it.

So naturally, I started telling everyone who'd listen.

"What if we tried this?" I'd say over lunch. "Wouldn't it be amazing if we could do that?" I was basically offering free consulting to the whole office, workshopping my idea out loud with anyone who'd engage.

I thought I was being collaborative. Building buy-in. Getting people excited about the possibility.

What I was actually doing was giving away my competitive advantage.

Three weeks later, I'm in a leadership meeting, and my colleague Jake is presenting an idea. MY idea. Wrapped in corporate speak and presented as his brilliant innovation.

I sat there watching him get praised for my concept, and I couldn't say a word. Because I had no documentation. No formal proposal. Just casual conversations that now made me look like I was trying to claim credit for his work.

That moment taught me something I wish someone had told me years earlier: your ideas need protection until they're ready to stand on their own.

And the painful part? This wasn't the first time it happened. I have this pattern of oversharing when I get excited about something. Like I can't hold onto an idea long enough to develop it properly before I start broadcasting it to everyone around me.

I did it with a retention strategy. Talked it through in team meetings for weeks. Then watched someone else present a "similar framework" they'd "been developing."

I did it with a process improvement. Casually mentioned it to a few people. Suddenly it was being implemented as someone else's suggestion.

I did it with a business opportunity. Shared too many details too early. The person I shared it with went directly to the prospect without me.

Every. Single. Time. I knew better. And I still did it.

I think it's because I get so excited about ideas that I want to share that excitement immediately. Or maybe I'm looking for validation that it's actually good. Or maybe I'm just not strategic enough to sit with something quietly until it's ready.

Whatever the reason, it kept costing me.

The worst part is how stupid I felt each time. Like, how many times do you need to learn the same lesson before you actually change your behavior?

Apparently, for me, the answer is "a lot."

What finally shifted things was getting absolutely burned on that project idea with Jake. That one stung enough that I couldn't ignore the pattern anymore.

So I made myself a rule: No sharing ideas until they're developed enough to be attributed to me. No workshopping concepts in public until I've written them down. No casual "what if we..." conversations until I'm ready to formally propose something.

It felt physically uncomfortable at first. Like I was being secretive or withholding. Like I wasn't being a team player.

But then something interesting happened. When I did finally present ideas, they landed harder. They had more impact. People took them more seriously because they were complete thoughts, not half-formed concepts.

And my name stayed attached to them.

I still mess this up sometimes. I'll get excited and start talking before I've protected the idea properly. But at least now I notice when I'm doing it. And sometimes I can catch myself mid-sentence and redirect.

"Actually, let me develop that more and bring it back to the group."

It's not perfect. But it's better than handing away my best thinking to whoever's in the room when inspiration strikes.

I'm telling you this because I see other women doing the same thing. Getting excited, sharing early, then watching their ideas get taken or their credit get diluted.

And I want to save you from learning this lesson as many times as I had to learn it.

Your ideas are valuable. Protect them until they're strong enough to survive attribution challenges.

Not because you're being secretive. Because you're being smart about what you've created.

4

LET SILENCE SPEAK

I'm sitting in my manager's office, and he just asked how I think I performed this quarter. Simple question, right?

Instead of answering, I word-vomited all over his desk.

I walked him through every project detail. Every small win. Every process I'd improved. I kept circling back because I was nervous, adding more and more context until my accomplishments sounded boring.

I watched his eyes glaze over in real time.

Later, I realized that if I'd simply said, "I reduced our critical vulnerabilities by 60 percent in six months," that would've been remembered. The details could've followed if he asked.

But I buried my power under a mountain of words.

We need to talk about something that's probably making you squirm a little right now.

Silence.

I know. Silence feels awkward. It feels empty. When there's a pause in conversation, your brain immediately starts scrambling to fill it. Someone asks a question and you feel compelled to give them your entire thought process, plus backup explanations, plus a few disclaimers just to be safe.

Sound familiar?

In the world of power, silence carries weight and creates presence. Saying less forces you to speak with precision so your words actually land.

Think about the last conversation you left wishing you'd kept your mouth shut. Did you overshare something personal? Did you explain your idea so thoroughly that it lost all punch? Did you add so many "maybe" and "I could be wrong, but" that nobody remembered your actual point?

Yeah. We've all been there.

We're not playing mind games here. We're giving our words the space they need to breathe and be heard.

Think about Michelle Obama. When she speaks, every word is deliberate. She doesn't ramble. She doesn't over-explain. She makes her point with clarity and then lets it sit there, powerful and complete.

That's the difference between speaking with power and speaking to fill space.

Women are conditioned to soften everything we say. To qualify. To apologize in advance. "I'm not sure if this is right, but..." or "This might be a stupid question, but..." or "I don't want to overstep, but..."

All those words before you even get to your actual point? They're eroding your authority with every syllable.

I had a colleague, Sarah, who was brilliant. Truly one of the smartest people I've ever worked with. But every time she presented an idea in meetings, she'd start with, "I was just thinking, and I could be totally wrong about this, but maybe we could consider..."

By the time she got to her actual suggestion, everyone had already mentally checked out. They heard the uncertainty in her preamble and tuned out the substance that followed.

We worked on it together. I challenged her to present her next idea with just one sentence. No qualifiers. No apologies. Just: "We should implement X strategy because Y."

The room went silent. Then someone said, "That's actually brilliant. Let's do it."

Same person. Same intelligence. Different delivery. Completely different result.

When you speak less, people sometimes interpret it as coldness or aloofness. Especially for women. We're expected to be warm, to over-explain, to make everyone comfortable.

But there's a huge difference between being brief and being cold. You can say less while still being warm. The key is in what you choose to say, not how much you say.

When someone asks how you're doing, "I'm great, thanks for asking" is warm and complete. You don't need to give them your life story to prove you care.

When someone questions your decision, "I've considered that, and here's why this approach works best" is confident and sufficient. You don't need to justify every thought that led you there.

The women who command respect in any room? They're not the ones talking the most. They're the ones who speak with such intention that everyone stops to listen.

I get it. You think more explanation equals more credibility, but the opposite is true.

I'm thinking of leaders like Jacinda Ardern, who became known for her clear, concise crisis communication. Or the late Ruth Bader Ginsburg, whose legal opinions were powerful precisely because every word earned its place. When they spoke, their words carried weight because they weren't wasted on filler. Every sentence had purpose.

When you master this skill, people start leaning in when you talk instead of tuning out. They remember what you said because you didn't bury it under unnecessary explanations. They respect your time because you respect theirs.

And you actually feel more powerful. When you stop trying to fill every silence, when you trust that your words are enough, you stand taller. You breathe easier. You own your space.

In meetings, resist the urge to be the first to speak. Let others fill the initial silence. When you do speak, make one clear point. Then stop. Don't add "Does that make sense?" or "What do you all think?" Just let your statement stand.

In emails, cut your drafts in half. I'm serious. Write your response, then delete every sentence that doesn't directly serve your purpose. You'll be shocked how much stronger the message becomes.

When giving updates to leadership, lead with the result. "We increased engagement by 22 percent." Period. If they want to know how, they'll ask. Don't bury your wins under process explanations.

In negotiations, state your position once. Clearly. Then let the silence do its work. The first person to fill that silence usually loses ground.

When you're in a leadership role, your team doesn't need your entire thought process. They need clear direction.

Try this: "We're targeting X. Here's the timeline. Questions about execution?"

Then stop. Leaders who speak with clarity and brevity build trust. Leaders who flood people with explanations create doubt about whether they actually know what they're doing.

People will try to bait you into saying more than you should. They'll ask leading questions or push for personal opinions in front of others.

The trap is filling silence with answers you don't owe anyone.

The stronger move? Say what serves the moment. Let the rest go.

I worked with Dana, a woman who had this habit of writing novel-length emails whenever there was even a hint of conflict. When a manager criticized her project, she responded with five long paragraphs of detailed explanations.

She thought she was protecting herself. Really, she was eroding her authority with every extra sentence.

She changed up and cut those responses down to three clear, professional sentences. Period. Done.

Within months, her reputation completely shifted. She went from being "the over-explainer" to "the woman who handles things efficiently."

Stop reading for a second. Think about your last email that was longer than it needed to be. What would happen if you'd cut it in half? Would anyone actually miss those extra sentences, or would your message have landed harder?

In your emails, try cutting one response in half. Strip out the fluff. Let your point stand naked and strong.

Notice your urge to fill silence in your next meeting. Don't. Sit in it for one beat longer than feels comfortable. Then make your point in one sentence and watch how people lean in.

These small moves will train you to trust the power of fewer words.

Saying less doesn't make you mysterious or cold. It makes you precise. It makes people remember what you said instead of drowning in what you could have said.

So the next time you feel that familiar urge to keep explaining, pause. Say the one thing that matters most.

Then let the silence do the heavy lifting for you.

Trust me on this one. Your future self will thank you.

CONTROL YOUR STORY
BEFORE SOMEONE ELSE DOES

Right now, someone is describing you in a conversation you're not part of. And that description is shaping opportunities you don't even know about yet.

Your reputation is both your armor and your invitation. It decides who trusts you, who doubts you, and who tries to push you aside.

And if you let your reputation get defined carelessly, you'll waste years repairing what you could have protected from the start.

Think of a moment when someone mischaracterized you. Maybe they called you "too emotional," "too ambitious," or "hard to work with." Notice how quickly those words travel.

They weren't describing your skills. They were trying to brand you. And once that brand sticks, it becomes truth in people's minds whether it's accurate or not.

Men in power understand this. They know that controlling the narrative about who you are gives them power over what opportunities come your way.

That's why you can't leave reputation up for grabs.

I worked with a woman early in my career who was brilliant at her job, but she made one critical mistake: she vented her frustrations openly in team meetings. Every time she disagreed with leadership, she let everyone see her irritation.

She thought she was being honest and direct.

Within a few months, she was labeled "difficult." That label followed her everywhere. When a promotion came up, leadership passed her over. Not because she wasn't qualified, but because her reputation had been defined by those emotional moments.

Meanwhile, another colleague had just as many concerns about leadership, but she handled it differently. She voiced her opinions strategically, in private conversations with solutions attached, never in ways that made her look reactive.

Her reputation? "Thoughtful. Strategic. A problem-solver."

Same frustrations. Different reputations. Completely different outcomes.

Your reputation comes down to one thing: what story people repeat when you're not in the room.

You also need to pay attention to the company you keep as it can impact your reputation as well. Watch how people handle pressure, how they treat rules when they think no one's looking, how they respond when things go wrong.

When someone consistently makes questionable choices, don't stand too close. When drama follows certain people everywhere they go, that's information. When someone always has an excuse for why nothing is ever their fault, that's a pattern.

A friend of mine got caught in this exact trap. She was loyal to a colleague who was constantly cutting corners and blaming others when things went wrong. She thought she was being a good friend by standing by him.

But when that colleague finally got called out for his behavior, her reputation took a hit too. Leadership started questioning her judgment. "If she can't see what kind of person he is, what else is she missing?"

It took her two years to rebuild that trust.

Here's what you need to do: Document your contributions to shared projects. Be clear about your role in writing. If someone tries to rewrite history later, you want proof of what actually happened.

And if you sense something's about to go sideways, get some distance. You don't have to throw anyone under the bus, but you also don't have to go down with their ship.

Protecting your reputation preserves your ability to do good work and help people in the future. That's not selfish. That's being strategic.

Stop and think: When people mention your name in rooms you're not in, what are the first three words you want them to associate with you? Professional? Trustworthy? Strategic?

Whatever those words are, every association you make either reinforces that image or chips away at it.

A healthcare administrator noticed that important decisions were happening in casual hallway conversations she wasn't part of. Instead of getting frustrated, she started positioning herself where these informal discussions happened.

Not to eavesdrop, but to contribute. When someone mentioned a difficult case, she'd offer a quick insight. When they discussed new protocols, she'd share relevant experience.

Soon, those same hallway conversations were building her reputation instead of diminishing it.

Think about those three words you want tied to your name. Keep them sharp. Then pick one daily action to back each up.

If "decisive," end your emails with a clear next step. If "steady," keep your tone level in tense meetings. If "innovative," contribute one fresh idea each week.

Over time, the reputation you choose becomes the reputation people repeat.

Your reputation will walk into every room before you do. If you craft it intentionally, it will do more talking for you than any speech ever could.

Guard your reputation like the precious resource it is. Because once it's damaged, rebuilding takes ten times more energy than protecting it would have in the first place.

BE VISIBLE

What's the most uncomfortable truth we'll face together?

You need to be seen.

Lol! I can feel you cringing. The idea of showboating or snatching the spotlight for attention sounds shallow, self-promoting, everything you were taught not to be.

But your brilliance is completely wasted if no one notices it.

At lunch one day, a colleague mentioned she kept getting passed over for promotions even though her results were flawless. When we talked about her presence in meetings, she admitted she rarely spoke unless someone asked her directly. I could only cringe. It brought me right back to the toxic advice my stepdad drilled into me: "Don't speak unless spoken to." It took me nearly twenty years to unlearn this.

Her logic? "If my work is strong enough, it'll be recognized."

If only the world worked that way.

Work doesn't speak for itself. People do. And people are influenced by what's visible, repeated, and memorable.

Once she started speaking up early in meetings and presenting her own projects instead of letting her manager take credit, everything changed. Within six months, she got the promotion she'd been chasing for two years.

Her skills didn't improve. Her visibility did.

I know what's running through your head right now. You've been conditioned to believe that drawing attention makes you arrogant, selfish, "too much."

Meanwhile, men are literally rewarded for doing the exact same thing. They interrupt. They restate obvious points. They claim credit for collaborative work. And instead of being criticized, they're seen as leadership material.

That double standard? It's real, it's exhausting, and you can either fight it forever or learn to work within it strategically.

I'm not telling you to become someone you're not. I'm telling you to make sure people actually see who you are.

There's a massive difference between attention-seeking and ensuring your contributions are visible. One is desperate. The other is strategic.

Think about the last time you delivered exceptional work. Who presented it? Who got the credit? If the answer isn't you, that's a visibility problem.

I once worked with a woman named Jessica who spent months developing a new client retention strategy. Brilliant work. But when it came time to present to leadership, her manager stepped in. "I'll handle the presentation," he said. "You did the hard work, I'll make sure they understand it."

She thought he was being helpful.

He got promoted three months later based largely on "his" strategy.

That's what happens when you let other people control your visibility.

In any professional environment, there are two levels of reality. There's the work you actually do, and there's what people think you do. Those two things are often completely different.

The work you do gets you results. What people think you do gets you opportunities.

You need both.

So how do you increase visibility without feeling like you're showing off?

First, own your presentations. If you did the work, you present the work. Period. Don't let anyone "take it from here" when it's time to share results with leadership.

Second, speak up early in meetings. Not just when you have the perfect point. Contribute early, even if it's building on someone else's idea. Early visibility makes people remember you were there.

Third, document your wins visibly. Send brief update emails to key stakeholders. Not bragging, just "Wanted to share that we hit X milestone on Y project." Keep it factual and frequent.

Fourth, volunteer for high-visibility projects. The ones that put you in front of senior leadership. Even if they're more work, the exposure is worth it.

I know someone's going to say, "But my work should speak for itself."

Here's what I wish someone had told me years ago. Your work does speak. The problem is, it's whispering while everyone else is using a megaphone.

You don't have to be the loudest person in the room. But you do need to be heard.

And we're not talking about taking credit for other people's work. We're talking about making sure you get credit for YOUR work. There's a massive difference.

When you contribute to a team project, make sure your contributions are visible. In team meetings, say "I handled X and Y." Not aggressively, just matter-of-fact.

In emails summarizing group work, make sure your name is attached to your specific deliverables.

In performance reviews, document everything you did with specifics.

Because if you don't claim your work, someone else will.

I've watched this happen too many times. A woman does the heavy lifting on a project. A man on the team presents it. Leadership assumes he did the work. She gets thanked for "supporting the team." He gets promoted.

And she's left wondering why her hard work never translates to advancement.

The difference is attention.

Think about the women you admire most in your field. The ones who've made it to leadership positions. I guarantee they didn't get there by staying quiet and hoping someone would notice their good work. They made themselves visible. They spoke up. They claimed credit. They showed up in ways that made them impossible to ignore.

Not because they're shameless self-promoters, but because they understood that visibility isn't vanity. It's strategy.

Your ideas deserve to be seen. Your contributions deserve recognition. Your voice deserves to be heard.

Draw attention not because you need applause, but because your ideas, your vision, and your influence deserve to be seen and remembered.

If you don't step into the light, someone else will drag your work into it with their name on it.

Attention isn't optional. It's the bridge between your talent and your opportunity.

Step into it with intention. Court it with confidence. And never apologize for being seen.

You've earned the right to take up space. Now take it.

STOP DOING EVERYTHING YOURSELF

I used to watch men climb corporate ladders built entirely on work they didn't even do, and it made me so angry.

They'd swoop in at exactly the right moment, present themselves as the visionaries behind projects that other people had poured their souls into, and get promoted for it.

Meanwhile, I was burning myself out trying to do everything myself because I thought that's what "earning it" looked like.

And I need to be honest about something: I was being an idiot.

Not noble. Not hardworking. Just strategically stupid.

I thought if I personally handled every deliverable, every detail, every piece of execution, then no one could question whether I deserved recognition. I'd have proof. I'd have evidence. I'd be undeniable.

What actually happened? I became invisible.

There was this major project I led. I did everything. The strategy, the research, the presentations, the implementation. I was there at 7 AM and left at 9 PM. I handled every crisis personally.

When it was time to present results to leadership, I showed them everything I'd accomplished. All the work I'd done.

You know what they said? "Great work. Who else was on this team?"

I said it was mostly me.

They looked uncomfortable. Like maybe I was exaggerating or taking too much credit.

Because leaders don't do everything themselves. Leaders direct work. They coordinate teams. They make sure things get done and their name stays visible on the outcome.

But I didn't understand that. I thought leadership meant doing the most work.

Meanwhile, my colleague Marcus was running a smaller project with half the complexity. But he'd delegated beautifully. He had three people contributing, and he made sure everyone knew he was leading them.

When he presented to leadership, he walked them through "his team's approach" and "his strategic vision" and "how he'd coordinated multiple stakeholders." He modeled leadership.

He got promoted. I got told to "work on developing others."

I was furious. But also, deep down, I knew they were right.

I wasn't leading. I was doing. And doing doesn't scale. Leadership does.

The painful part is how long it took me to change this. Even after that experience, I kept falling into the same trap. Taking on too much. Refusing to delegate because I thought it would be faster to just do it myself.

I told myself I was being thorough. Really, I was being afraid.

Afraid that if I wasn't personally doing the work, I wouldn't deserve the credit. Afraid that delegating meant I was lazy. Afraid that if I led instead of executed, someone would figure out I didn't belong in leadership.

It took burning out completely before I finally got it.

I ended up taking time off because I couldn't function anymore. And during that forced pause, I watched my team keep working without me. Projects moved forward. Deliverables got completed. The world didn't fall apart.

They didn't need me to do everything. They needed me to direct things. To remove obstacles. To make strategic decisions.

When I came back, I tried something terrifying: I delegated a major presentation to someone on my team. The kind of presentation I would normally have spent three weeks perfecting myself.

I coached her. I gave her the strategic framework. I reviewed her work. But she built it and she delivered it.

And it was great. Maybe even better than if I'd done it myself because she brought a fresh perspective I wouldn't have had.

That's when I finally understood: delegation isn't weakness. It's multiplication.

Now I focus on direction, not execution. On strategy, not tactics. On making sure the work gets done and my leadership is visible, not on doing everything myself.

And you know what? I'm better at my job now. And less exhausted. And more likely to actually get promoted because I'm showing leadership skills instead of just worker bee skills.

But I'm still fighting that instinct. That voice that says "it'll be faster if I just do it myself" or "I need to prove I can handle this personally."

That voice is a liar. And listening to it almost destroyed my career.

So yeah. I spent years doing it wrong. Learning the hard way that working harder doesn't equal working smarter.

I'm telling you this so you don't waste as much time as I did trying to earn leadership through exhaustion instead of through actual leadership.

8

STOP CHASING, START ATTRACTING

The moment you start chasing people, whether it's for approval, opportunities, or respect, you've already handed over your power.

I used to be the queen of this mistake. Early in my career, I was that person sending follow-up emails before anyone had even had time to read the first one. I'd volunteer for everything, say yes to every request, and basically make myself so available that people stopped valuing my time entirely.

There was this one project where I was desperate to prove myself to a senior director. I kept scheduling meetings with him, sending him updates he didn't ask for, basically throwing myself at this opportunity like my career depended on it.

And you know what happened? He started avoiding me. My eagerness made him see me as needy rather than capable.

That's when a mentor pulled me aside and said something that changed everything: "When you chase people, you're teaching them that you're less valuable than they are."

Think about Beyoncé for a second. She doesn't chase record labels or beg for collaborations. She creates something so undeniable that the entire industry comes to her. That's not arrogance. That's understanding your worth and positioning yourself accordingly.

But women are conditioned to be accommodating, to make things easy for everyone else, to always be the helpful one. Society tells us that being accessible and eager is a virtue.

Meanwhile, men take their time responding to emails. They say things like, "Let me check my calendar and get back to you." They create scarcity around their time, and somehow that makes everyone respect it more.

The difference is, they were taught early that their time has value. We were taught that our worth comes from how much we give to others.

So I completely flipped this dynamic. I stopped answering emails immediately. Not to be rude, but to signal that I had priorities and boundaries. I started saying, "I'm reviewing several options for this project and will have a recommendation by Friday." Instead of presenting every half-formed thought, I'd come to meetings with one clear, well-researched position.

The shift was incredible. People started preparing more carefully before they brought things to me. My calendar became respected instead of assumed. My opinions carried more weight because I wasn't handing them out like free samples.

Your value grows when your presence becomes intentional rather than constant.

When you're always available, always eager, always the first to volunteer, people subconsciously think: "She must not have anything better to do. She must need this more than we do."

But when you position yourself as someone with options, with standards, with boundaries? They start thinking: "I need to get on her calendar. I need to make sure she chooses us."

I knew a woman in sales who was pitching herself into complete exhaustion. Always chasing prospects. Always lowering her prices before anyone even asked. Always offering extra services to "prove her worth."

She looked desperate. And desperation repels opportunity.

She eventually reframed her entire approach. Instead of chasing, she started positioning herself as selective. She created compelling case studies of her biggest wins and shared them strategically. She started using phrases like, "I only work with companies ready for this level of transformation."

Within three months, the entire dynamic flipped. Prospects were asking her for a spot on her calendar. She wasn't begging for meetings anymore. She had become the person they wanted to reach.

Running after people makes them see you as lesser. Standing still, grounded in your value, makes them cross the room toward you.

Here's how you actually implement this without coming across as difficult or aloof:

First, create genuine value that people actually need. The goal isn't to play hard to get. It's to be genuinely in demand because you're that good. Develop an expertise that's rare. Deliver results that are undeniable. Build a reputation that precedes you.

Second, set boundaries around your time. Stop responding to every request within minutes. Stop saying yes to every meeting invite. Your immediate availability signals that you have nothing more important going on.

Third, let others pursue you occasionally. When someone asks for your time, it's okay to say, "I'm booked solid this week, but I can make time next Tuesday if that works." You're not being difficult. You're treating your calendar like the valuable resource it is.

Fourth, demonstrate selective interest. You don't have to chase every opportunity that comes your way. When you're selective, people wonder why you're passing on certain things. That curiosity makes them value your yes even more.

The goal isn't to become unavailable or difficult. It's to become so valuable that your time and expertise are treated with the respect they deserve.

Stop running after opportunities, approval, and attention. Stand confidently in your expertise and let people come to you.

You're not playing hard to get. You're being authentically valuable.

And when you position yourself that way, the whole dynamic shifts. You're no longer the one asking for a seat at the table. You're the reason the table exists in the first place.

9

LEAD WITH RESULTS
NOT DRAMA

Okay, I need to be direct with you about something.

You're wasting your breath arguing with people, and it's making you look worse, not better.

I know that's harsh. But someone needs to say it.

You can debate until you're blue in the face, and most of the time, the other person just digs in deeper. All that energy you're spending trying to convince people with words? It's not working.

So here's a better way: Stop arguing. Show them instead.

I'm thinking about every time I've watched you get defensive when someone questions your approach. You launch into this whole explanation, trying to prove you're right, talking faster and faster until everyone's eyes glaze over.

And the person who questioned you? They walk away thinking you're defensive and insecure, not capable and strategic.

Words create friction. Results create conviction.

When you argue, you're inviting people to find holes in your logic, to question your judgment, to dig in their heels. But when you deliver measurable outcomes? There's nothing left to debate.

My former director got into a massive argument with her peer about the best approach for a new initiative. She was probably right, but she spent three meetings trying to convince him through pure debate.

He kept pushing back. She kept arguing harder. It became this whole thing.

Finally, she changed tactics. She said, "Let me run a pilot and show you the results."

Three weeks later, she presented data showing a 23% improvement in their key metric. He couldn't argue with that.

Same idea. Different approach. And this time it actually worked.

I'm not saying you should never explain your thinking. Sometimes context helps. But there's a massive difference between brief context and exhaustive defense.

Brief context: "Based on our Q2 data, I recommend we shift resources to digital channels."

Exhaustive defense: "Well, if you look at the data, and I know the sample size isn't huge, but it does show a trend, and I've been thinking about this for weeks, and I consulted with three different people who agree..."

Which one sounds more confident?

When you need to disagree with someone powerful, don't make it about being right. Make it about testing an approach. "I'd like to test this with a small pilot. Can we review results in 30 days?"

Shift from debate to demonstration.

And honestly? Sometimes you need to let people be wrong. Not every hill is worth dying on. Not every incorrect statement needs your correction.

Pick your battles based on: Does this actually affect outcomes? Or are you just arguing because you want to be right?

If it's the second thing, let it go. Save your energy for the battles that matter.

Look, I know you've been trained to prove yourself with words. To show your work. To demonstrate your thinking process. But that training is making you less effective, not more.

The most powerful people I know don't explain everything. They deliver results that speak louder than any explanation could.

Stop trying to win arguments. Start delivering outcomes that make arguing irrelevant.

Your work either proves you right or it doesn't. Words won't change that.

So next time you feel that urge to defend yourself, to explain, to justify? Pause. Ask yourself: What could I show them instead?

Then go show them.

Because at the end of the day, results don't argue back. They just win.

And when your work speaks that loudly, you won't need to say another word.

10

PROTECT YOUR ENERGY FROM TOXIC PEOPLE

You know exactly who I'm talking about, don't you?

The chronic complainer who finds you at every coffee break. The drama magnet who somehow always has a crisis that becomes your emergency. The colleague who turns every conversation into a therapy session about how unfair life is.

We've all had them in our orbit. And if you're anything like me, you've probably felt guilty for wanting to run the other way when you see them coming.

Energy is contagious. The people you spend time with don't just influence your mood, they shape your reputation, your opportunities, and your entire trajectory.

Confidence, stability, and joy will lift you higher. But chaos, insecurity, and constant negativity? They'll infect you if you let them get too close.

And as women, we're often expected to be the emotional caretakers everywhere we go. At work, at home, in our social circles. That expectation can trap you in cycles where you're constantly giving your energy to people who don't want to heal, they just want an audience for their misery.

I worked with someone early in my career, Linda, who was brilliant at her job, but she was also perpetually miserable. Every Monday morning, she'd corner me with stories about how everything was falling apart. Her marriage. Her manager. Her entire life.

At first, I thought I was being a good friend by listening. Offering advice. Trying to help her see solutions.

But you know what actually happened? I started absorbing her stress. I'd leave those conversations feeling drained and anxious. And worse? Other people started associating me with Linda's negativity.

When a high-visibility project came up, my manager passed me over. Later, I found out why. "You seem like you have a lot going on right now. I need someone fully focused."

I didn't have a lot going on. But Linda's drama had become my reputation by proximity. I paid a personal price for accommodating her issues.

That's when I learned: you can't save people who don't want to be saved, and trying will cost you everything you're working toward. No one is entitled to rob you of your energy and capacity to lift yourself.

I'm not telling you to become cold or to abandon people who are genuinely struggling. There's a massive difference between someone going through a hard time and someone who weaponizes their misery.

Someone going through a hard time? They're working on solutions. They appreciate your support. They reciprocate when you need them.

Someone weaponizing misery? They reject every solution you offer. They're offended if you don't want to hear the same complaints for the hundredth time. They drain you and give nothing back.

You need to learn to tell the difference.

I started protecting my energy without feeling like a terrible person by setting time boundaries. Instead of open-ended conversations that could spiral for an hour, I'd say, "I have ten minutes before my next call. What's going on?" That automatic timer kept me from getting trapped.

I stopped offering solutions to people who weren't interested in solving anything. If someone complained about the same issue three times without taking any action, I'd say, "That sounds really frustrating" and change the subject. No more free therapy sessions.

I started noticing patterns. People who only called when they needed something but disappeared when I needed support? I let those relationships fade.

And I got intentional about who I spent time with. I started seeking out people who energized me. Who celebrated wins. Who talked about possibilities instead of problems.

The shift was incredible. My stress levels dropped. My reputation improved. And honestly? I became more effective at my job because I wasn't carrying everyone else's emotional baggage.

Think about your own circle right now. Who leaves you feeling lighter after you talk to them? Who makes you feel heavier?

Make a mental list. Then ask yourself: am I spending more time with the people who lift me up or the people who drag me down?

If the answer makes you uncomfortable, it's time to make some changes.

You're not responsible for managing other people's emotional stability. You're responsible for protecting your own.

That doesn't make you selfish. It makes you smart.

I had someone tell me once, "I'm running the emotional concession stand for dramas I didn't even want to watch."

That's exactly what happens when you keep engaging with other people's instability. You become part of their act. Step out of the tent. Let the circus continue without you.

Instability spreads. Misery truly does love company. And if you don't draw clear lines, you'll find yourself repeating their complaints, echoing their drama, and carrying burdens that were never yours to begin with.

You deserve so much better than that.

Your energy is your most valuable asset. It determines what you can create, who you can become, and how far you can rise.

So choose circles that feed your growth, not drain your spirit. Because nobody rises when they're carrying anchors tied to other people's chaos.

Your peace is your power. Guard it fiercely, and don't hand it over to anyone who refuses to guard their own.

11

BECOME THE GO-TO, NOT THE FALL-BACK

You know what's worse than being overlooked? Being the person everyone thinks of last, especially when their first three choices fell through.

I watched this happen to a colleague who was genuinely talented. Excellent problem-solver, reliable, competent. But she'd become the "backup plan" person. The one managers called when their preferred expert was unavailable. The one who got asked to help after everyone else had already passed.

She thought being helpful would advance her career. Really, she was training people that she was the fallback option, not the first choice.

And if you're not someone's first call when they need your kind of expertise, you don't have as much power as you think you do.

There's a massive difference between being useful and being essential. Useful people are nice to have around. Essential people are the ones projects wait for. The ones whose calendars everyone works around. The ones who get pulled into rooms because decisions can't be made without their specific expertise.

The women who actually have power? They're not the ones who do everything. They're the ones who do specific things so exceptionally well that people seek them out by name.

Think about your current role. When people need your particular skillset, are you their first thought? Or are you the person they remember exists after they've already tried someone else?

Be honest with yourself here. That answer tells you everything about where your power actually sits.

Simone was a data analyst I used to work with. She got stuck being everyone's backup. She could analyze anything, run any report, clean up any messy spreadsheet. But because she said yes to everything, she became generic in people's minds. Just "someone who's good with data."

Then she made a strategic shift. She stopped taking every data request that came her way and started specializing. Customer behavior analysis. That was her thing. She got deep into it, learned advanced techniques, built custom models, became the person who could predict customer patterns nobody else saw.

Within six months, she wasn't the backup analyst anymore. She was the customer behavior expert. Marketing wouldn't launch campaigns without her input. Product wouldn't make decisions without her analysis. Her calendar was booked weeks out because people knew they needed her specific expertise, not just "someone who does data."

Same person. Same underlying skills. Completely different positioning.

That's what becoming the go-to instead of the fallback actually looks like.

We're not talking about making people dependent on you to manipulate them. We're talking about building genuine expertise that creates real value. Value so clear and specific that when people need what you do, they think of you first. Not because you've withheld information or made yourself artificially necessary, but because you're genuinely excellent at something specific.

There's a crucial difference. Manipulation creates resentment. Excellence creates respect.

A project manager figured this out after years of being the "she'll handle it" person. She did everything: timeline management, stakeholder communication, risk assessment, budget tracking, team coordination. She thought being versatile made her valuable.

Instead, it made her replaceable. Because "does everything adequately" is less powerful than "does this one thing exceptionally."

She picked one thing to master. Cross-functional project coordination for technical launches. That specific, complex skillset that sits at the intersection of technical teams, business stakeholders, and customer needs. She got so good at it that when the company had a critical product launch, they wouldn't start without her leading the coordination.

That's strategic positioning. Not manipulation. Not withholding. Just genuine expertise in something specific that matters.

So how do you actually build this kind of value?

Start by identifying what you're actually exceptional at. Not what you can do. Not what you're decent at. What are you genuinely better at than most people around you? That's your foundation.

Then get even better at it. Deepen that expertise. Learn the advanced techniques. Understand the nuances. Become the person who sees things in that domain that others miss.

But you can't fake this. You can't position yourself as an expert without actually building real expertise. People see through hollow claims quickly.

A software developer told me she watched a colleague try to brand himself as "the AI expert" by talking about AI constantly, sharing articles, using the buzzwords. But when people actually came to him with AI implementation challenges, he couldn't deliver. His reputation crashed faster than it had been built.

Real expertise takes time, focus, and genuine skill development. But that investment pays off exponentially when you become the person people actually need, not just the person who's available.

So pick your territory. Build genuine mastery. Say no to things that dilute your focus. Make yourself so good at your specific thing that when people need it done right, you're their first call, not their fall-back option.

Stop being useful for everything. Start being essential for something specific.

Because the woman who's everyone's backup has very little power. But the woman who's someone's first and only choice for something critical? She controls her calendar, her rates, and her career trajectory.

WHEN TO SHARE AND WHEN TO HOLD BACK

Greene's original version of this is about how historical figures used selective honesty to manipulate people. Like, share a small truth to make them trust you, then use that trust to control them. Some people interpret his research, which is a history lesson, as advice for how to treat people. That's dangerous. And we're not doing that.

But there's something in there worth pulling apart. Something about understanding that not everyone deserves your full honesty.

And that sentence right there makes me squirm because I've always believed authenticity is everything. That being real, being transparent, being open is how you build genuine connection.

But what if that's naive?

Let's test this. An erratic homeless person walks up to you on the sidewalk and shouts "Give me some money. How much money you got?" Do you: A) tell him "I've got $300 cash and 3 credit cards," B) open your wallet while concealing its contents as you pull out a dollar, or C) say nothing and go on your way?

POWER TALKS BULLSH*T WALKS

If we're being honest, most people don't go full disclosure. That's selective honesty. Not everyone is entitled to know your truth if they haven't earned your trust. And you're not obligated to put yourself in harm's way for the sake of honesty.

But here's where it gets complicated: When does protecting yourself cross the line into manipulating others?

The Framework: Where Strategic Honesty Becomes Manipulation

I've thought about this a lot, and I think the line comes down to these criteria:

Strategic honesty is ethical when:

- Both people benefit from the outcome, not just you
- You're willing to be vulnerable too, not just extracting their vulnerability
- You're building a real relationship, not just getting what you need and disappearing
- Everything you share is true. You are choosing what to share, not lying
- You're protecting yourself from harm, not positioning to harm them
- They have equal choice to share or not share

It crosses into manipulation when:

- Only you benefit from the exchange
- You weaponize what they share against them later
- You fake vulnerability to extract real vulnerability from them
- You deliberately hide information they need to make fair decisions

- You're extracting power or leverage over them
- They're exposed while you stay protected

Let me show you what this looks like in practice.

Story 1: When I Learned the Hard Way

Once upon a time I was completely transparent with a new colleague. Shared my concerns about a project. Talked about my frustrations with how leadership was handling something. Just being honest, you know? Treating her like I'd want to be treated.

Two weeks later, she used everything I'd said in a meeting to position herself as more aligned with leadership than I was. Made me look like the problem.

Here's what I got wrong: I didn't vet her first. I gave her access to information that could be weaponized before I knew whether she was trustworthy. The mistake wasn't being honest. It was being honest too soon with someone I hadn't assessed yet.

She crossed the line. She used what I shared for one-sided gain and weaponized my openness against me. Classic manipulation.

The lesson: Build trust incrementally. Share small things first and see what people do with that information before you share bigger things. Professional honesty until someone proves they deserve more.

Story 2: When Strategic Vulnerability Worked

There was this situation at work where I needed to build trust with a department head who was blocking one of my initiatives. I could have come in all facts and logic. Instead, I shared something real, a mistake I'd made early in my career that was related to what we were discussing.

It opened her up. She shared something similar. We connected. And then she was willing to reconsider her position.

Was that manipulation? Let's run it through the framework:

- ✓ Mutual benefit: Unblocking the initiative helped both of us and the project
- ✓ Reciprocal vulnerability: She shared back, and I didn't use what she said against her
- ✓ Real relationship: We continued working together productively afterward
- ✓ Truth-based: Everything I shared was genuine
- ✓ Protective intent: I was building a bridge, not extracting leverage
- ✓ Equal choice: She could have stayed closed off; I wasn't forcing anything

This was strategic, yes. But it was ethical. The vulnerability was real, the intention was mutual benefit, and the outcome served everyone involved.

The lesson: Strategic vulnerability can build genuine trust when your intention is connection and mutual benefit, not extraction and control.

Story 3: When I Saw Someone Cross the Line

I watched a colleague share a "vulnerable" story about living out of his car while homeless to build sympathy in an interview with the director for a position he was less qualified to fill than others. This story had no relationship to the interview questions or demonstrating competency for the position.

51

He later repeated this story publicly to the director's senior manager in casual conversations leading up to the hiring decision. A month later, the director selected him for the promotion over higher qualified women that interviewed. She later told the stunned candidates management decided to go in a different direction with no further explanation provided. Once hired for the position, he never told the story again.

That's manipulation and a perfect example of how men play these games. I'm still steamed about it when I think about it.

He:

- ✓ Benefited at everyone else's expense
- ✓ Weaponized vulnerability (with a story no one could validate)
- ✓ Faked intimacy to garner sympathy to overshadow his lack of qualifications
- ✓ Used his knowledge of the director's soft spot for helping kids
- ✓ Created a situation where the risk was one sided. If she passed over him, she would feel guilty and risk going against her superior's preference for him

When I see that kind of behavior, I know exactly what it is: calculated manipulation disguised as connection.

So Where Does This Leave Us?

Your full story isn't for everyone. Your deepest truths aren't public property. And choosing who gets access to what isn't dishonesty. It's wisdom.

Here's how to practice selective honesty ethically:

1. Vet people before you trust them. Watch what they do with small information before you give them big information.

Do they keep confidence? Do they use what you share to help or harm you?

2. Ask yourself: Who benefits? If the answer is "only me," pause and reconsider. Ethical strategic honesty creates mutual benefit.

3. Be willing to be vulnerable in return. If you're only taking information and never giving it, that's extraction. Real relationship building is reciprocal.

4. Never weaponize what people share. If someone trusts you with something real, honor that. The moment you use their honesty against them, you've crossed the line.

5. Check your intention. Are you building connection or extracting advantage? If you can't have the conversation without a specific outcome, you might be manipulating.

6. Share truth, just not all of it at once. Selective honesty means choosing what and when to share. It doesn't mean lying, fabricating, or creating false impressions.

The people who've earned your trust get your real honesty. Everyone else gets professional honesty, polite, appropriate, and protective. And there's nothing wrong with knowing the difference.

Selective honesty means being deliberate about who gets to see the real you. That's not hiding. That's protection.

And when done with the right intention and ethical boundaries, that's not manipulation. That's survival.

13

FRAME EVERY REQUEST
AS COLLABORATION

You know that knot in your stomach when you need to ask for help? That voice in your head whispering, "You should be able to figure this out yourself"?

Yeah, I see you. And I need to tell you something that might surprise you.

That hesitation? It's not protecting your credibility. It's sabotaging it.

One of the trickiest dynamics you face is asking for help. You either avoid it completely because you don't want to seem weak, or you swing the other direction and apologize your way through every request until you sound like you're begging.

Both approaches are killing your power.

Asking for help isn't weakness. People actually like being asked because it makes them feel valuable and influential. But if you ask the wrong way, you create an imbalance where they feel you owe them, where they can use your request as leverage, or where your credibility takes a hit.

One of my most cringe-worthy professional moments involved needing support from a senior colleague on a complex project. But I was terrified of looking incompetent.

So I stumbled into her office saying things like, "I'm sorry, I probably should know this already, but could you maybe help me with..." By the time I finished that train wreck of a sentence, I'd already discredited myself.

When I stepped back and analyzed what went wrong, I realized I needed to completely reframe my approach. The next time I needed help, I walked in and said, "I'd love your perspective on this strategy because your expertise will make my approach much stronger."

Notice the difference? The first version sounded apologetic and weak. The second version honored her strength while keeping my authority completely intact.

She helped me gladly and respected me more for how I asked.

Every request you make can either drain your power or reinforce it. The difference is entirely in your framing.

Men have mastered this instinctively. They rarely apologize for asking. They frame requests as opportunities: "I'll need your input here" or "You'll want to be part of this."

Meanwhile, we're softening our asks until they disappear entirely.

The shift is simple but radical. Stop apologizing for needing support. Start framing it as collaboration.

Think about how Mary Barra navigates complex stakeholder negotiations at GM. She doesn't approach unions, the board, or government officials asking for favors. Instead, she positions every request as mutual benefit. That's not manipulation. That's understanding human psychology.

People don't help because you need them. They help because helping serves them in some way, whether that's feeling valuable, building influence, or creating future opportunities.

So instead of saying: "I hate to bother you, but could you possibly..."

Try: "Your experience with X would really strengthen this project. Can I get your input?"

See how that works? You're not begging. You're offering them a chance to contribute their expertise to something meaningful.

Instead of: "I'm sorry, I know you're busy, but I was wondering if maybe..."

Try: "I'm working on something that aligns perfectly with your strengths in Y. Can we schedule 20 minutes?"

You're respecting their time by being specific, and you're honoring their expertise by naming exactly why you're asking them.

Now let's talk about when people try to weaponize their help against you. Some people, often men in positions of influence, will "help" you in ways that come with invisible strings attached.

They'll remind you of favors. Make you feel indebted. Expect your silence or loyalty in return. That's manipulation disguised as generosity.

You'll know it's happening when their help feels heavier than the original problem.

Your response? Clear boundaries. When someone tries to hold help over your head, you can say, "I really appreciate your support. The project turned out so much stronger because of your input." Period.

Gratitude closes the loop. It doesn't sign you into emotional servitude.

You've probably been trained to over-thank people. Endless thank-yous, guilt-driven payback, shrinking in their presence because they "did you a favor."

Gratitude is healthy. Indebtedness is disempowering. Learn the difference.

Think about where you've been making yourself small when asking for help. What phrases do you use that give away your power?

Next time you need to ask for something, try this. Instead of apologizing or over-explaining, honor the person's strength and show how their input connects to something bigger. Something like: "Your experience with contract negotiations would really strengthen this proposal."

Frame it with respect, not apology. Notice how differently people respond when you approach them as a collaborator rather than a supplicant.

I once told someone, "Asking for help doesn't make you weak. Asking badly makes you weak."

No one succeeds alone. Men understand this. They ask constantly, but they never frame it as neediness. They frame it as leadership.

You can and must do the same.

Ask for help without owing anyone your dignity. Frame your requests in ways that build respect, protect your authority, and keep your independence intact.

The way you ask matters as much as what you ask for. Frame it with strength and watch how the entire dynamic shifts in your favor.

14

STRATEGIC LISTENING

Okay, so I need to talk about this principle because the original version makes me want to throw the book across the room.

It's basically about pretending to be someone's friend so you can spy on them and gather intelligence. Like some corporate espionage nonsense where you're manipulating people into trusting you just so you can use their information against them.

That's disgusting. That's sociopathic. And I'm not doing it.

But here's what's making me angry: the fact that this is how some people actually operate. And we're supposed to just smile and pretend everyone's motivations are pure while they're playing these games behind our backs.

I've had coworkers who posed as friends while clearly gathering ammunition. They'd ask detailed questions about my challenges, my frustrations, my vulnerabilities. And then those exact things would come up later in ways that hurt me.

"Just being concerned." "Just checking in." Meanwhile they were building a file.

And the really infuriating part? When you call it out, you look paranoid. "She's not a team player." "She doesn't trust people." "She's closed off."

No, I'm just paying attention to patterns. I'm noticing that every time I share something real with this person, it gets weaponized against me later.

But somehow I'm the problem for noticing?

So yeah, I'm uncomfortable with this whole principle. But I can't just ignore it because pretending this behavior doesn't exist doesn't protect me from it.

Here's what I'm willing to extract from this mess: Information does flow through relationships. The colleague who mentions budget cuts are coming. The mentor who shares which projects leadership actually cares about. The peer who reveals that a difficult client is finally ready to make a decision.

That information helps you make better choices. And being aware of it, paying attention to it, that's not manipulation. That's just being strategic about understanding your environment.

The difference is intention and reciprocity.

If you're building genuine relationships and information flows naturally through them? That's fine. That's how professional networks work.

If you're pretending to care about someone specifically to extract information you can use against them? That's manipulation. And it's gross.

I'm so tired of watching people operate this way and getting rewarded for it while the rest of us try to have actual integrity.

So here's what I'm going to do instead: I'm going to build authentic relationships with people I genuinely respect. I'm going to be curious about my environment. I'm going to pay attention to what I learn through those relationships.

But I'm not going to pose as anyone's friend. I'm not going to pretend I care when I don't. And I'm not going to use people's trust against them.

And when I sense someone doing that to me? When someone's asking unusually detailed questions about my challenges, or pumping me for information about other colleagues, or clearly fishing for things they can use?

I'm going to protect myself. Warm smile. Professional boundaries. And zero access to anything real.

Because I've been burned enough times to know: some people use friendship as a weapon. And recognizing that isn't being cynical. It's being awake.

Information is valuable. Authentic relationships are even more valuable. But fake relationships designed to extract information?

Those are toxic. And I refuse to participate in that game.

15

CUT OFF TOXIC POWER
AT THE ROOT

We need to talk about something you've been avoiding.

You know that person in your life who keeps undermining you? The one who says they're "just being honest" when they tear you down? The colleague who steals your ideas or the manager who somehow makes every conversation about your failures?

You've been trying to manage around them. Telling yourself they'll change. That you should be the bigger person and just ignore it.

I need you to hear this: hoping toxic people will magically transform is like hoping weeds will turn into roses. It's not going to happen.

And every day you spend hoping is a day you're letting them damage you.

This calls for you to do something surgical: Cut off toxic power at the root.

I don't mean destroy the person. Dismantle their ability to hurt you.

And I know what you're thinking. "But I don't want to be that person. I don't want to be mean. Maybe if I just..."

Stop. Right there.

You're not being noble by tolerating abuse. You're not being mature by letting someone sabotage you. You're being afraid to protect yourself. And that fear is going to cost you your career if you don't wake up.

Toxic dynamics rarely fade on their own. When you try to "manage around" manipulative people, tolerate their behavior, or hope they'll soften over time, they usually come back more emboldened.

Power works like weeds. Trim the surface and they grow back stronger. Pull the root and they can't return.

I'm thinking of that situation you're in right now. You know exactly what I'm talking about. You've been trying to be patient. To give them the benefit of the doubt. To avoid conflict.

And what's happening? It's getting worse, not better.

So here's what you're going to do:

Identify the real root. Is the problem gossip? Their influence over key people? Emotional manipulation? Don't waste energy fighting symptoms. Go straight to the source.

Use evidence, not emotion. Document behaviors, patterns, outcomes. Your feelings give them ammunition to call you "too sensitive." Hard evidence takes their power away.

Create strategic distance. Stop giving access to people who've proven they'll misuse it. Limit interactions. Set clear boundaries. Request reassignment if necessary.

Close the loop completely. Once you've cut the root, don't keep circling back. Don't try to fix the relationship or give them second chances. That only reopens wounds.

I know someone's going to say "But that seems harsh. What about giving people grace?"

Here's my response: You've already given them grace. Multiple times. And they've used that grace to hurt you more.

Grace doesn't mean letting someone repeatedly damage you. That's not grace. That's just poor boundaries dressed up as virtue.

You don't have to destroy people to protect yourself. But you absolutely have to stop toxic power before it destroys you.

Some battles aren't worth fighting. This one is.

So stop waiting for them to change. Stop hoping it'll get better. Stop being the bigger person while they're actively working against you.

Cut the root. Protect yourself. And move forward without them.

You needed to hear this.

16

STOP BEING SO AVAILABLE

I'm going to tell you about the most exhausting phase of my career, and how it almost destroyed everything I'd built.

I became my company's designated "fixer." Any crisis, any last-minute disaster, any impossible deadline? They called me.

At first, I was flattered. They trust me. They value me. I'm indispensable.

I'd stay late to handle emergencies that poor planning created. I'd answer emails at 11 PM. I'd cancel personal plans when someone needed something. I was available 24/7, and I wore that like a badge of honor.

For about six months, I felt like a superhero. Then I started noticing something unsettling.

Nobody was noticing my brilliance anymore. They weren't seeing my strategic thinking or my innovative solutions. They were just seeing my availability. I'd become office furniture: always there, always functional, completely taken for granted.

When I delivered excellent work, the response was basically "thanks." When I missed one late-night emergency because I was sick, people were annoyed. How dare I not be available.

I was invisible. Not because I wasn't talented, but because my talent had become background noise. My constant presence made everything I did feel ordinary instead of exceptional.

Then I found out I'd been passed over for a promotion. I was devastated. I asked my manager why.

His response? "We need someone who can think strategically, not just handle operations."

I wanted to scream. I WAS thinking strategically. But nobody saw it because they only called me for firefighting, and I always said yes.

My constant availability had typecast me as the reliable workhorse instead of the strategic leader.

That's when I realized: if you're always available, your presence becomes meaningless.

So I started an experiment that terrified me. I set boundaries. Real ones.

No more late-night emergency emails unless someone was literally dying. No more rescuing every crisis created by other people's poor planning. No more being available 24/7.

When someone would ask me to handle an urgent situation, I'd check whether it was actually urgent or just poorly planned. If it was the latter, I'd say "I can help you with this next week, but I'm at capacity right now."

At first, I was terrified they'd see me as not committed. Not a team player. Not valuable.

The opposite happened.

Leadership started seeing me differently. They respected my time more. When I did step in to help, my impact was actually noticed because it wasn't constant background noise.

And the best part? Someone else stepped up to handle those constant emergencies. Turned out, when I stopped being available for everything, other people had to develop their own problem-solving skills.

Within three months, I got pulled into strategic planning conversations I'd never been invited to before. Within six months, I got the promotion I'd been passed over for.

Nothing changed about my actual capabilities. I just stopped diluting them with constant availability.

I think about that phase now and realize how close I came to burning out completely. How much damage I did to my career by making myself too accessible.

And I see other women doing the exact same thing. Being the ones who always say yes, always stay late, always pick up the slack. Thinking it makes them valuable when really it makes them invisible.

Your value doesn't come from being always available. It comes from being impactful when you choose to show up.

Strategic absence makes your presence more powerful.

I'm not saying become unavailable or difficult. I'm saying protect your time like the valuable resource it is. Because when you're constantly accessible, people stop appreciating you and start expecting you.

And expectation without appreciation is just exploitation with a smile.

17

DON'T BE SO EASY TO READ

You know that friend who shares every detail of her life? Every plan, every worry, every strategy? She thinks she's being authentic and transparent. But what's really happening is she's making herself incredibly easy to manipulate.

Power slips away the moment people think they've got you completely figured out. When they can predict exactly how you'll react, what you'll decide, or where you'll move next, they'll use that roadmap to control you.

A colleague from my former company prided herself on being an "open book." She thought transparency was her superpower. Everyone knew her career goals, her timeline for applying to promotions, even her deepest insecurities about her qualifications.

She felt authentic. Connected. Real.

But there was this male colleague who wanted the same promotion she was eyeing. Because she had shared everything, he knew exactly when she planned to apply, exactly what she'd highlight in her pitch, and exactly where she doubted herself.

He beat her to the punch. Applied two weeks before her planned timeline. Used the same talking points she'd workshopped out loud. Even addressed the very concerns she'd voiced about her readiness.

She thought openness was her strength. Really, she'd handed him a detailed playbook for how to outmaneuver her.

When you're too readable, other people start writing your story for you.

Women are taught that men aren't. We're supposed to be open, vulnerable, emotionally available at all times. Authenticity, we're told, means sharing everything. Being "real" means having no boundaries around what we reveal.

Meanwhile, men are taught to play their cards close. To keep their strategies private. To reveal only what serves them. And when they do it, it's called "being strategic." When we do it, we worry we're being "fake."

Strategic privacy doesn't make you fake, It protects your agency.

Think about how Angela Merkel navigated sixteen years as German Chancellor. She was famously hard to read. Colleagues called her the "sphinx" because she revealed so little of her internal process. That unpredictability? It was part of her power.

Or look at how Christine Lagarde operates at the European Central Bank. She's strategic about what she reveals and when. She protects her decision-making process while maintaining public presence.

When you're too easy to read, several things happen.

People know exactly which buttons to push to manipulate you. If you always react to criticism with visible hurt, they'll use that. If you always say yes when asked directly, they'll exploit it.

Your competitors get advance notice of your moves. When you talk through your goals before they're ready, you give others the chance to interfere, copy, or block you.

You lose negotiating power. If people know your exact bottom line, your fears, your desperation, they'll use it against you.

Your emotions become weapons others can use. When people can predict your exact emotional response, they can trigger it on command.

Don't always react the same way to similar situations. When people can predict your exact response, they can manipulate it.

Maintain some professional mystery. You don't need to share every thought process or decision-making method.

Vary your patterns occasionally. If you always say yes immediately, sometimes pause. If you always respond within minutes, sometimes take longer.

This doesn't mean becoming cold, distant, or manipulative. It means protecting the parts of yourself that need protection while remaining warm and professional.

Once someone knows your rhythm completely, they can trap you in it.

Think about where you're too easy to read right now. Maybe you always say yes immediately when someone asks for help. Maybe you wear every emotion so plainly that people know exactly which buttons to push. Maybe you talk through your goals before they're ready, giving others the chance to interfere.

What part of you would be stronger if you kept it closer until the right moment?

The next time you feel the urge to over-explain, don't. Stop two sentences earlier than you normally would. Leave some space. Notice how people respond when you don't hand them every detail.

The goal isn't to create fear or confusion in others. The goal is to protect your own agency and decision-making power.

You don't need to become a mystery, but you also don't need to hand out spoilers before your story is written.

Strategic privacy isn't coldness. It's protection.

The woman who can't be fully predicted is the woman who can't be fully controlled.

Protecting your next move doesn't make you secretive. It makes you strategic.

Your plans belong to you until you decide to reveal them. Guard them. Protect them. Let others see your results, not your entire process.

Because the moment people can predict every move you'll make, they stop respecting the moves you do make.

18

STAY CONNECTED, BUT BE PICKY

I keep going back and forth on this thing.

After everything we've talked about, like reading people and protecting yourself and cutting off toxic power, there's this voice in my head saying I should just lock myself away from everyone. Build walls. Trust no one. Become some kind of workplace hermit.

And part of me finds that appealing, honestly. No drama. No risk. No getting burned by people who turn out to be something other than what they seemed.

But I also know that's a trap. Because the moment you wall yourself off completely, you become irrelevant. And irrelevant people don't get opportunities or advance or change anything.

So I'm trying to figure out: where's the line between protecting yourself and isolating yourself?

When someone pulls back at work to avoid the drama or politics, it feels like the smart move. But the downside is people start to forget you're there.

If you stop showing up, stop chatting, stop being part of things, your work can fade into the background. And when promotions or opportunities come around, it's usually the people who stayed visible who get noticed, not necessarily the ones who were the most qualified.

The consequences? You can protect yourself right out of relevance.

So complete isolation clearly doesn't work. But neither does being everyone's best friend and saying yes to everything, because that's how you end up like Tara who became the office emotional dumping ground. Every crisis, every venting session, every "can you just quickly" request landed on her until she burned out so badly she had to take medical leave.

Both extremes are destructive. But I'm still trying to figure out what the middle actually looks like.

I think it's about selective access. You're not a community center that has to be open to everyone all the time. But you're also not a fortress that keeps everyone out.

Some people deserve your time and energy. Others don't.

The problem is figuring out which is which before you get burned.

Maybe the answer is: start with professional friendly to everyone, then let people earn deeper access over time through their behavior.

Not their words. Their behavior. Do they respect your boundaries? Do they reciprocate when you help them? Do they keep information you share confidential? Do they have your back when you're not in the room?

Those behaviors earn access. Everything else gets pleasant professionalism.

I don't have a perfect answer for this. But what I'm pretty sure about is this: you need allies to survive in any workplace. You need people who know your value, who'll speak up for you when you're not in the room, who'll give you the heads up when someone's gunning for you.

If you wall yourself off completely, you lose all of that.

But you also can't be everyone's person. You can't say yes to every request, answer every text, listen to every complaint. That's how you end up exhausted and resentful.

So maybe the answer is: build a core group of genuinely trusted allies, and invest there. Be professionally friendly with everyone else. Say no without guilt when requests don't align with your goals. Show up strategically, not everywhere.

I'm testing this approach now. Three people I genuinely trust and invest real time with. Everyone else gets pleasant, professional, boundaried interaction.

And you know what? It's working better than either extreme ever did.

I'm not isolated. But I'm also not drowning. I have allies when I need them, but I'm not carrying everyone else's stuff.

Maybe that's the balance. Not walls, but filters. Not isolation, but intention.

I'm still working this out. But I think maybe the goal isn't to figure out the perfect formula. The goal is to stay flexible enough to adjust based on who people actually show themselves to be.

Start open enough to build connections. Get selective based on behavior. And don't feel guilty for having boundaries just because someone else wants more access than they've earned.

That's not being cold. That's being wise.

19

KNOW WHO YOU'RE CHALLENGING (SOME PEOPLE DON'T FORGIVE)

You're being your authentic self, speaking your truth, maybe even standing up for what's right. And then BAM! Someone who seemed totally fine with you before is suddenly making your life hell.

Sound familiar? Because I'm willing to bet it's happened to you more times than you want to count.

Remember when we talked about protecting your independence and setting boundaries? Well, this goes hand in hand with that. Because all the boundaries in the world won't help you if you can't tell the difference between someone who'll respect them and someone who'll see them as a personal attack.

Here's a cautionary tale about a woman that was a brilliant strategist. She worked on major infrastructure projects. She had this habit of calling out bad ideas in meetings. It didn't matter who suggested them. One day she told a city councilman his infrastructure proposal was "completely divorced from reality."

He smiled. Nodded. Even thanked her for her "candid feedback."

Six months later, when budget time came around, guess whose department got slashed? She thought she was being brave. Really, she'd just painted a target on her back.

I'm not saying you should become some fake, people-pleasing version of yourself. But there's a difference between being authentic and being reckless.

Some people can handle directness. They'll argue with you, maybe even get heated, then buy you a drink afterward. Others? They'll smile sweetly while mentally adding your name to their revenge list.

The tricky part is that the dangerous ones often don't look dangerous. They're not the ones throwing tantrums in meetings. They're the ones who go quiet when challenged, who remember every slight, who wait for the perfect moment to strike back.

You know who I'm talking about. You've met them. That colleague who never seems to get upset about anything, until suddenly they're telling your boss you're "difficult to work with." The friend who always acts supportive but somehow your opportunities keep disappearing.

Some people's egos are like landmines. You can't see them until you step on one.

Women get into trouble here because we've been told to be honest, to speak up, to not hold back. And yes, those things matter. But nobody warned us that some people will punish us for years over one moment of perceived disrespect.

Men seem to understand this instinctively. Watch how they navigate their bosses' egos, how carefully they deliver bad news to powerful people, how they frame disagreements as collaborative problem-solving rather than challenges.

Meanwhile, we're out here being "refreshingly direct" and wondering why our careers hit invisible walls.

Some people need to be right more than they need to be effective. Challenge their ideas publicly and they'll make it their mission to prove you wrong, even if it hurts the whole organization.

Some people collect grudges like trading cards. They'll smile and nod when you contradict them, then file it away for the perfect revenge moment months or years later.

Then there are the people who see disagreement as personal attack. Their professional identity is wrapped up in being smart or being right, and any challenge feels like you're calling them incompetent.

And some people have more power than you realize. That "peer" who seems harmless might be the CEO's college roommate or the board member's daughter. Cross them carelessly and you'll learn about invisible power the hard way.

The key is learning to spot these patterns before you step in them.

Watch how people react when others challenge them. Do they engage intellectually or do they get defensive? Do they argue in the moment or do they quietly retaliate later?

Pay attention to who has informal power. The executive assistant who schedules all the important meetings, the finance person who controls budget approvals, the IT director who can make your life miserable with "technical difficulties."

Notice who holds grudges. Some people will tell the same story about being wronged five years ago like it happened yesterday. That's your warning sign.

And before you speak, ask yourself: Is being right here worth making an enemy? Sometimes yes, sometimes no. But at least make it a conscious choice.

So what does this look like in practice?

When you need to disagree with someone powerful, do it privately first. Frame it as seeking their wisdom: "I want to understand your thinking on this because I'm seeing some data that seems to conflict."

When you have to correct someone publicly, give them an out. "That's a great point, and I wonder if we should also consider..." Same message, totally different impact on their ego.

And when someone shows you they're vengeful, believe them. Don't assume you'll be the exception. Protect yourself accordingly.

It's not about being fake. It's about being effective. Because what good is being right if it costs you everything you're working toward?

The woman who can read a room, who knows when to push and when to step back, who understands that not every hill is worth dying on, she's the one who actually gets things done. She's the one who changes things without becoming a casualty of someone else's bruised pride.

Stop martyring yourself on the altar of being right. Not every battle is worth fighting, and not every person is safe to cross. Sometimes the wisest move is walking around the obstacle, not charging straight through it.

The woman who sees others for exactly who they are rather than who she wishes they were will always move further with less damage.

Clarity isn't just about knowing yourself. It's about seeing others with sharp, honest eyes and protecting your path by choosing carefully who you cross and when.

Because in the end, it's not just about being right. It's about being effective.

20

PROTECT YOUR YES

So I finally figured out why I'm constantly overwhelmed despite thinking I'm good at saying no.

And it's embarrassing how long this took me to see.

I spent weeks feeling like I was drowning. Too many commitments, too many projects, too much on my plate. But every time someone asked me to take something on, I'd consider it carefully and say no to anything that didn't align with my goals.

I was being so strategic! So boundaried! So protective of my time!

Except I was still exhausted and overwhelmed and making no progress on anything that actually mattered.

Then my friend Briana pointed out what I couldn't see. I was good at saying no to things I didn't want to do. However, I was terrible at saying no to things that didn't help me achieve my goals even though they made me look impressive.

Oh.

She was right.

I'd turn down random requests and committee work and low-value projects. But then I'd volunteer to organize the office charity drive. And join two new cross-functional initiatives. And mentor three junior employees. And take on a stretch project that would "look great on my review."

Different sources of drain. Same result: no energy left for what actually mattered.

I thought saying no to bad opportunities was enough. But I was still saying yes to too many mediocre opportunities dressed up as impressive ones.

And here's the thing: all of those commitments sounded good when I said yes. Organizing the charity drive made me look like a leader. The cross-functional initiatives connected me with other departments. Mentoring showed I invested in others. The stretch project demonstrated ambition.

But cumulatively? They were destroying my ability to do anything with real impact.

I was scattered across ten different things instead of concentrated on the two things that would actually move my career forward.

And I couldn't see it because each individual yes seemed justified. It was the collective weight I wasn't calculating.

Women especially fall into this trap because we're socialized to believe that saying yes makes us likeable, that availability equals professionalism, that being helpful is how we prove our worth.

So we say no to things we don't want and feel proud of our boundaries. Then we turn around and say yes to five other things that look good on paper but drain us just as much.

I had to start asking a different question. Not "Do I want to do this?" or "Will this make me look good?" but "Where does this lead me?"

Because a lot of impressive-sounding opportunities lead nowhere except to being impressively busy.

Organizing the charity drive? Kind of me and showed leadership, but it had zero connection to my actual career goals.

One of the cross-functional initiatives? Interesting but tangential to my core work.

Mentoring three people simultaneously? Generous but unsustainable.

The stretch project? Actually aligned with where I wanted to go, so that one stayed.

Everything else? I had to let go, even though they made me look good. Even though saying no made me feel guilty. Even though I worried people would think I wasn't a team player.

And you know what happened when I consolidated down to just the commitments that actually aligned with my goals?

I started making real progress. Not just looking busy. Actually building something meaningful.

But I'm still fighting this instinct. Last week someone asked me to join a committee that would "great exposure." And my immediate reaction was yes because exposure sounds important.

Then I caught myself. Exposure to who? For what purpose? Leading where?

I couldn't answer those questions clearly, which meant this was another impressive-sounding distraction.

So I said no. And it felt terrible because the opportunity sounded good and I worried about what they'd think of me for declining.

But you know what feels worse than saying no to impressive-sounding opportunities? Saying yes to so many of them that you never actually accomplish anything meaningful.

I'm learning, slowly, that being selective isn't the same as being selfish. That protecting my yes from good opportunities so I can save it for great opportunities isn't lazy or uncommitted.

It's just finally being strategic about where my limited energy actually goes.

But I'm not going to lie, it's still hard. That voice that says "but this would look so good" is loud and persistent.

I'm just trying to make sure the voice that says "but does this serve where I'm actually going" is louder.

PLAY THE STUDENT,
NOT THE EXPERT

Look, the original version of this power principle is disgusting. It reflects how certain historical figures pretended to be ignorant to manipulate and control people. That's not what we're doing here.

Despite its dark tone, there's something valuable buried in that mess we can learn in a more positive manner: the power of strategic listening and making others feel heard.

And this is where women have a secret advantage if we're willing to use it strategically instead of apologetically.

My friend Lisa is incredibly smart. I mean like, *intimidatingly* smart. But she was totally stuck with this one manager who kept shooting down her ideas. Every meeting was the same: she'd come in with the perfect plan, explain it clearly, and then watch him pick it apart and say no all over again.

I finally asked her, "What if you let him think he's teaching you something?"

Next meeting, instead of presenting her solution, she started with questions. "Help me understand how you've been approaching this." "What's worked well for you in the past?" "Where do you see the biggest challenges?"

The guy talked for forty minutes straight. And in the process, he basically outlined exactly what he needed, which happened to be exactly what Lisa had been trying to give him all along.

But now it felt like his idea. When she offered her "suggestions" to build on his insights, he practically jumped across the table to shake her hand.

Same brilliant solution. Completely different delivery. She didn't play dumb. She played curious. And curiosity is strategic intelligence disguised as humility.

If you're dealing with a boss or client who tends to dismiss your ideas, try shifting your approach from pitching to collaborating.

Instead of presenting your idea right away, start by asking about their experience:

"I'm working through this challenge, and I know you've handled something similar before. How did you approach it?"

Listen carefully and ask follow-up questions to show genuine interest in their perspective. Once they've explained their thinking, build on it:

"That makes a lot of sense. What if we used that same approach but tweaked it a bit for this situation?"

By framing your idea as an extension of theirs, you invite collaboration rather than confrontation. The end result is the same idea—just with a lot more buy-in.

Women have been socialized to listen, to ask questions, to make space for others' voices. Men are taught to assert, to claim, to dominate conversations. So when we use strategic listening, there's always this fear that we're just playing into old stereotypes about women being passive or deferential.

But there's a massive difference between listening because you think that's all you're allowed to do, and listening because you're smart enough to gather intelligence before you make your move.

The beautiful thing about this approach? You're not diminishing yourself. You're amplifying the other person while strategically positioning your ideas for maximum acceptance.

People don't just respect your intelligence. They trust your judgment. And trust opens doors that raw intelligence alone never could.

Here's how this actually works in practice:

Start with genuine questions, not leading questions designed to trap someone, but real curiosity about their perspective and experience. Listen more than you speak. Aim for a 70/30 ratio. Let them talk 70% of the time while you listen actively.

Reflect back what you hear. "So what I'm hearing is..." This shows you're paying attention and gives them a chance to clarify.

Build on their ideas. Frame your suggestions as extensions or refinements of what they've shared, not contradictions.

Give credit generously. When your idea succeeds, acknowledge their contribution. "This wouldn't have worked without your insight about..."

The woman who makes others feel smart becomes the woman everyone wants on their team. Not because she's actually less intelligent, but because she's wise enough to know that influence requires more than being right. It requires making others feel valued.

You have to actually listen. Not just wait for your turn to talk. Really listen. Be genuinely curious about their perspective, even when you think you already know the answer.

That curiosity isn't weakness. It's reconnaissance. It's how you learn what people really care about, what they're afraid of, what would make them look good.

And once you know that? You can position your brilliance in a way that serves their needs while advancing your goals.

That's not manipulation. That's mastery.

22

KNOW WHEN TO PIVOT, KNOW WHEN TO WALK AWAY

Listen, I need to tell you something that might sound completely backwards after everything we've talked about.

Sometimes the most powerful move is to pivot or walk away.

I know that feels wrong. We've spent all this time talking about boundaries and standing your ground and not letting people push you around. But there's a difference between fighting battles you can win and wasting your life on battles that are already lost.

And you need to learn to tell the difference.

I watched a colleague destroy herself trying to win a fight she couldn't win. She was in this brutal battle with our division head who had it out for her. Every proposal she made got shot down. Every project she led got micromanaged into the ground.

For months, she fought back. More data. Longer emails explaining her reasoning. Meetings to defend her decisions. It was exhausting just to witness.

Then something shifted. She just stopped. Stopped defending herself in meetings. Stopped trying to convince the division head she was right. Stopped caring whether this guy thought she was brilliant.

Instead, she redirected all that energy into building relationships with other department heads, volunteering for cross-functional projects, networking with senior leadership outside her division.

Six months later, she got offered a director position in a different part of the company with better pay and way more autonomy.

Her former nemesis? Still stuck in the same role, still creating drama nobody wanted to deal with.

She won by walking away from a fight she couldn't win and putting her energy where it could actually make a difference.

That's what strategic surrender really means. It's not giving up. It's redirecting your power toward where it can actually work.

And I need you to hear this: not every battle deserves your energy. Some fights are designed to drain you, to keep you so busy defending yourself that you can't build anything new.

The people who want you to stay trapped in those fights? They're counting on you being too stubborn to walk away.

But walking away isn't defeat. It's strategy.

You've tried everything reasonable and nothing changes. If you've communicated clearly, offered solutions, made genuine efforts, and the situation stays toxic, it's not going to magically get better.

The fight is draining more than it's building. If defending your position costs more energy than the position is worth, you're losing even if you eventually "win."

Your opponent wants the fight more than the resolution. Some people enjoy conflict. They're not interested in solving problems. They want the drama. Don't give it to them.

Sometimes winning this battle loses you the war. Sometimes being right about one thing costs you relationships, opportunities, or credibility that matter more in the long run.

Stop martyring yourself on battles that don't deserve you. Not every fight is worth your energy.

Surrender isn't the end. It's the reset. The woman who knows when to pull back and preserve herself will always outlast the one who burns out trying to win everything.

Letting go isn't weakness. It's wisdom. The win comes not from the battle you avoided, but from the strength you saved for the one that matters.

FOCUS YOUR ENERGY
WHERE IT MULTIPLIES

You know what's fascinating? We just talked about the power of walking away, and this is basically the flip side of that same coin.

When you let go of fights you can't win, you free up energy to concentrate on the ones you absolutely can dominate.

But most women get this completely backwards.

I was chatting with a friend about her career frustrations. She's exhausted, overwhelmed, and feeling invisible despite working constantly. When I asked her to walk me through her typical week, I started seeing the problem immediately.

She's on four different committees. She volunteers for every company initiative. She mentors half the junior staff. She's networking with three different professional groups. She says yes to every speaking opportunity, every panel, every "quick coffee."

On paper, she looks incredibly involved. In reality, she's accomplishing nothing meaningful anywhere.

Compare that to a colleague, James. He focuses on exactly three things: his core customer relationships, one high-visibility project that showcases his expertise, and building deep connections with two key decision-makers in his company. That's it.

Guess who just got promoted?

Women are told that being helpful, being visible, being involved is how we prove our value. So we show up everywhere, volunteer for everything, support everyone. We think that's what makes us indispensable.

Meanwhile, men focus ruthlessly on the three things that actually matter to their advancement. They guard their time, concentrate their efforts, and build reputations on a few well-chosen wins.

This isn't about working less. It's about working with surgical precision instead of scattered desperation.

Think about how Sundar Pichai built his career at Google. He didn't try to lead every initiative or be visible in every meeting. He concentrated his force around a few critical projects: Chrome, Android, Google Drive. He did them so exceptionally well that he became irreplaceable.

When you focus like a laser, everything you do starts reinforcing everything else. Your reputation becomes clear. Your expertise becomes undeniable. Your value becomes obvious.

But when you scatter yourself across ten different priorities, you're basically invisible in all of them. You're the person who's "pretty good at a bunch of stuff" instead of the person who's "absolutely essential for this specific thing."

And guess which one gets promoted?

Here's what you need to do:

Identify your core strength. What are you genuinely excellent at? Not just competent, but excellent. That's your foundation.

Choose one or two areas to dominate. Not five. Not ten. One or two. Where can you become known as THE person for this thing?

Say no to everything that doesn't multiply that focus. You'll have to turn down opportunities that sound interesting, impressive, or lucrative. Do it anyway.

Pour resources into your chosen area: time, money, energy, connections. Everything goes toward building undeniable expertise in your focused domain.

Let other things go. Actively. Deliberately. Some things that used to matter won't matter anymore. That's not failure. That's strategy.

Think about where you're currently spreading yourself thin. What would happen if you pulled back from 80% of those commitments and went twice as deep on the remaining 20%?

I'm willing to bet you already know which activities actually multiply your core goals and which ones just keep you busy.

Stop trying to do it all. Women are encouraged to "have it all" and "do it all," but doing it all is a trap that keeps you exhausted and invisible.

You don't have to be everywhere. You only have to be in the right places, with the right focus. That's where your strength multiplies.

The woman who tries to do everything becomes forgettable. The woman who focuses on one thing exceptionally well becomes irreplaceable.

Choose where you'll focus. Then pour everything into it.

24

BE VALUABLE WITHOUT BEING THREATENING

Think of Tyrion Lannister in Game of Thrones. He survived kings, queens, and family members who literally murdered people, all because he mastered the art of being valuable without being threatening.

Tyrion navigated the deadly politics of King's Landing by being indispensable while never making anyone feel diminished by his intelligence. He read every room, knew exactly what each powerful person needed to hear, and adjusted his approach accordingly, which is literally why he kept his head while others lost theirs.

Every workplace has its own version of King's Landing.

Nobody tells you about climbing in your career that the technical skills that got you hired are only about 30% of what determines your success. The other 70%? Understanding the political environment you're in and knowing how to navigate it.

Every company, every department, every team has its own power structure. Its own unspoken rules. Its own culture about who gets listened to and who gets ignored. And if you can't read those dynamics and adjust accordingly, all the brilliance in the world won't save you.

I learned this the hard way when I switched companies mid-career. At my previous job, I'd been known for speaking up in meetings, challenging ideas, pushing back when I disagreed. It worked beautifully there. Leadership loved it. They said I brought "fresh perspective" and "wasn't afraid to ruffle feathers."

Then I joined a new company and brought that same energy.

It was a disaster.

In this new culture, direct challenge was seen as disrespectful. Speaking up without being invited was considered aggressive. The women who succeeded here were the ones who built consensus quietly, who influenced through one-on-one conversations before meetings, who framed their ideas as questions rather than declarations.

I wasn't reading the room. I was trying to play by the rules of my last employer. Different employer. Different rules.

A mentor finally pulled me aside and said, "You're brilliant, but you're making people defensive. You need to learn how this place actually works before you try to change it."

That was my wake-up call. I had to become a student of this new environment. Watch how decisions really got made. Notice who had informal power versus official titles. Understand which battles mattered and which were symbolic.

Learn to read what people actually value, not what they say they value.

Every workplace claims to value innovation, boldness, fresh thinking. But watch what actually gets rewarded. Some places reward the person who comes up with ideas. Other places reward the person who executes flawlessly. Some cultures promote the person who builds strong relationships. Others promote whoever delivers numbers.

Pay attention to what actually works in this specific environment, not what theoretically should work.

If you want to build trust and influence with a new leader or decision-maker, start by observing before you act. Spend the first few weeks, or months if you can, watching how they work. Notice what they value and what makes them say yes or no.

Once you understand their priorities, tailor your approach to fit them. For example, if they care deeply about preparation and data, don't show up with half-baked ideas. Come with well-researched proposals, supporting documents, and answers to the questions they're likely to ask.

Keep testing your ideas from every angle before you present them. When you show that you've done the work and understand what they need to feel confident, you stop being just another person with opinions. You start becoming the person they rely on.

But you have to be valuable without making anyone feel threatened by your value.

The key is finding ways to be brilliant while making other people feel smart. To influence decisions while letting leaders feel like it was their idea. To solve problems while giving credit generously.

Think about how Satya Nadella transformed Microsoft. He inherited a company known for cutthroat internal competition and aggressive leadership. But he built his influence by making space for collaboration, asking questions, and empowering others. He had this gift for making every team feel like their work mattered to the bigger vision.

And in the process, he became one of the most successful CEOs in tech history.

That's high-level political intelligence. He built his influence by making space for others to feel powerful in his presence.

You're not changing who you are. You're changing how you deliver who you are based on what will actually land in this specific environment.

Your values stay the same. Your integrity stays intact. Your goals don't shift. But your approach adapts to the political reality you're navigating.

When I finally figured this out, I started asking different questions in new situations. Who really makes decisions here? Often not the person with the title. What does this leader need to feel confident saying yes? What are the unspoken rules about how ideas get heard? Who has informal influence, and how did they build it? What mistakes have I seen other people make in this environment?

These questions helped me decode each new political landscape I entered.

Build relationships across power levels, not just up.

I watched a woman named Claudia master this. She was an executive assistant, which many people dismissed as a support role. But Claudia understood something crucial: she had access to the CEO's calendar, knew which projects he cared about, could get her requests prioritized.

The smart people in our company? They built relationships with Claudia. They asked her advice before approaching the CEO with ideas. They made sure she knew how their work connected to his priorities.

The people who ignored her because she "wasn't senior enough"? They struggled to get face time with leadership and couldn't figure out why.

Claudia had real power in that system. She wasn't senior on the org chart, but she was indispensable to how things actually worked. And she used that position to help people who respected what she brought to the table.

Stop trying to succeed using the rules from your last environment. Every new team, every new boss, every new company has its own political ecosystem. Your job is to study it before you try to change it.

Watch for how people actually get promoted here. What mistakes get punished versus forgiven. Who gets listened to in meetings, and why. What kind of communication style does leadership respond to. Where is the real power in this organization.

And then adapt your approach accordingly.

You're not selling out. You're not being fake. You're being strategic about how you deliver your authentic brilliance in a way that will actually be received.

Because the most talented people don't always rise. The people who rise are the ones who combine talent with the political intelligence to navigate the specific environment they're in.

Think about your current workplace. What are the unspoken rules about power that you haven't been paying attention to? I'm willing to bet there are at least three dynamics you've been overlooking because you were too focused on doing good work instead of understanding how work actually gets valued in this specific place.

Understanding that every environment has different rules and learning those rules before trying to rewrite them, is what separates women who survive from women who thrive.

You don't need a royal court to practice this principle. You just need to remember that every room you enter has its own power dynamics. And your job is to read them accurately before you try to reshape them.

25

STOP LETTING OTHERS DEFINE YOU

We've been talking about navigating political environments, reading power dynamics, making yourself indispensable. But there's something underneath all of that, that we need to address. Something that might be holding you back more than any external obstacle.

The story you're telling yourself about who you are.

Because after years of watching brilliant women stay stuck, I've noticed something. If you don't actively define yourself, someone else will do it for you. And their definition will always be smaller than what you're capable of.

They'll box you in with labels. "She's the detail person." "She's great with people but not strategic." "She's reliable but not leadership material." And if you accept those labels, you'll spend your life bumping up against ceilings they built for you.

Women get labeled and boxed in faster than men do. Because people are comfortable with us in certain roles. The helpful one. The organized one. The supportive one. When we try to break out of those boxes, there's resistance. Not because we're not capable, but because our expansion makes people uncomfortable.

A graphic designer I knew was great at what she did and became known as the "logo girl." She was brilliant at branding and amazing at clean corporate design. But every time a big creative campaign came up, agencies would bring in someone else to lead the concept.

She was frustrated, but she'd also internalized their story about her. She'd introduce herself as "the one who makes brands look professional" instead of "the one who helps brands connect emotionally with their audience." She was reinforcing their box every time she opened her mouth.

Then something shifted. Maybe she got tired of being overlooked for the exciting projects, or maybe she just decided she wanted more. She started pitching big creative concepts, not just polished execution. At first, clients looked surprised. This wasn't the version of her they knew.

But she kept showing up differently. Started a blog about emotional design. Created spec campaigns that showed her range. Built a portfolio that proved she could think strategically, not just execute beautifully. Slowly, people's perception shifted. Within two years, she was creative directing campaigns for major brands.

Same person. Same talent. But she'd reinvented how she showed up in the world.

This connects to everything we've talked about. Remember when we discussed focusing your energy? Sometimes the most important asset to focus on is your own sense of identity. When you're clear about who you are and what you bring, everyone else gets clear too.

Reinvention doesn't mean transforming into an entirely new person. It means letting go of the old versions of yourself that no longer work for where you're going.

Maybe you're still thinking of yourself as "the hobbyist" when you're ready to be the professional. Maybe you're still introducing yourself as "just starting out" when you have years of experience. Maybe you're still playing in the minor leagues because that felt safe, but now it's just limiting.

I see this especially with women in creative industries who started in supporting roles. You were the amazing assistant, the reliable coordinator, the person everyone could count on to make things happen behind the scenes. But now you're ready to be the one creating the vision, not just executing someone else's.

That transition requires active reinvention. You have to start showing up differently before people will see you differently.

Think about how Ava DuVernay transformed herself from a publicist into one of the most influential directors in Hollywood. She didn't wait for permission to call herself a filmmaker, she started making films and became one.

Or look at how Tory Burch went from being known as "a fashion insider's wife" to building a billion-dollar fashion empire. She refused to let other people's limited view of her define what she could create.

Each reinvention built on the last one, but neither woman stayed stuck in any single version of herself.

So look at how you introduce yourself at industry events or in professional settings. Are you still leading with old roles or limiting descriptions? That's where this starts.

Instead of "I do wedding photography," try "I capture life's most important moments." Instead of "I write romance novels," try "I create stories about human connection." Instead of "I'm just the analyst," try "I turn data into insights that drive decisions."

Same work, different frame. You're not lying, you're expanding how people see your value.

The resistance you'll feel to this? That's normal. Change feels uncomfortable, even when it's change you want. Part of you will whisper that you're being pretentious or overreaching.

You're not. You're finally telling the truth about what you're capable of.

And women apologize for their own evolution. "I used to be in admin, but now I'm trying this leadership thing..." Stop. You're not "trying" anything. You're doing it. Own it.

Think about how you currently describe yourself professionally. What limiting language are you using? What outdated version of yourself are you still presenting to the world? I'm willing to bet there's at least one phrase you use regularly that's underselling who you've become.

Who do you need to become to get where you want to go? What aspects of your current identity are holding you back from that vision? Not who you should become according to someone else's expectations, who you actually want to become.

Take how you introduce yourself in three different contexts: networking events, your bio, and team meetings. Focus on the value you create, not just the tasks you perform. The difference between "I manage social media accounts" and "I build engaged communities that drive business growth" is enormous. Both are true. One opens doors.

The beautiful thing about reinvention is that you don't need anyone's permission to start. You don't need a new title, a promotion, or external validation. You just need the courage to let go of who you used to be and step into who you're becoming.

Because your identity isn't fixed. Your potential isn't limited by your past. And the story you tell about yourself today doesn't have to be the same story you tell tomorrow.

The woman who actively shapes how others see her is the woman who gets to choose her own trajectory.

Stop waiting for others to recognize your evolution. Start showing them who you're becoming.

26

BE SELECTIVE ABOUT WHO YOU WORK WITH

You know what nobody warns you about when you're building your career? How fast someone else's mess can become your problem.

I'm talking about the colleague who's always late on deadlines. The team member who overpromises in presentations and underdelivers. The coworker who talks badly about everyone behind their backs. You think you're just working alongside them, doing your part, staying in your lane. But when the reputation hits fly, proximity matters.

Actually, you've probably already experienced this. Remember group projects in college? There was always that one person who didn't pull their weight. Maybe they showed up to one meeting out of five. Maybe they volunteered to do the research but turned in three half-baked paragraphs the night before it was due. Maybe they just disappeared entirely and you had to scramble to cover their section at the last minute.

And when you presented that project to the class and it wasn't great? The professor didn't just grade the slacker poorly. Your whole group got dinged. Even though you stayed up until 3 AM trying to salvage their part. Even though you did twice the work you signed up for.

You all got the same B-minus, and that grade went on everyone's transcript.

That's your first lesson in guilt by association. And it doesn't stop after graduation. It just gets way more expensive.

There was a very talented woman named Lauren who worked hard and built a solid reputation in her department. Then she got assigned to a big project with this guy Tom. Nice enough guy. Fun to grab lunch with. Also completely unreliable when it came to actually doing the work.

Lauren saw it early on. He'd miss deadlines, then ask her to cover for him in meetings. He'd promise the client things without checking with the team first. He'd show up unprepared and wing it, leaving her to clean up the confusion later. But she didn't want to be that person, you know? The one who complains, who isn't a team player, who makes things difficult. So she worked twice as hard to compensate and kept her mouth shut.

The project ended up over budget and behind schedule. The client wasn't happy. And when their manager asked what went wrong, guess whose name came up in the conversation? Both of theirs.

Lauren had met every single one of her deadlines. She'd done excellent work. But she'd been standing close enough to Tom's mess that some of it stuck to her anyway.

It took her almost a year to shake that association. A year of people hesitating before adding her to important projects, wondering if she was reliable. All because of six months working next to someone who wasn't.

That's what I need you to understand. Your reputation isn't just built on what you do. It's built on who people see you doing it with.

Remember when we talked about owning your identity? Well, you can't protect an identity you don't guard. You can shape how you show up all day long, but if you keep aligning yourself with people who have questionable judgment, you're fighting an uphill battle.

And women catch more heat for this than men do. When a guy on a team drops the ball, people blame him individually. When you're on a team that fails, people question your judgment for being part of it in the first place. It's not the same standard, and it's not fair. But it's real.

I think about situations I've seen where a woman joins a committee or working group, and later finds out the person running it has a reputation for being disorganized or difficult. Suddenly, she's associated with that chaos by proximity. People start wondering about her judgment: "Why would she align herself with that?"

Or you know that coworker who's always in some kind of conflict? Always has drama with someone? Maybe they're even justified sometimes. But after a while, people just start avoiding anyone associated with them because they don't want to get pulled into it.

I watched this happen with a colleague who volunteered to co-chair a company diversity initiative. Her co-chair seemed passionate about the cause, which was great. But this person also had a habit of sending aggressive emails, calling people out publicly in meetings, and generally burning bridges while trying to make change happen.

My colleague wasn't doing any of that. She was trying to build consensus and work diplomatically. But because their names were on everything together, she started getting feedback that she was "too confrontational" and "not collaborative enough." She was being judged by association, not by her actual behavior.

When she finally requested to step down and work on a different initiative, she had to spend months rebuilding relationships and proving that she could, in fact, work well with others.

So you can support people without tying your reputation to their patterns. You can be kind without being naive. You can be a team player without signing up to clean up someone else's recurring messes.

Pay attention to the patterns. Does this person consistently miss deadlines? Do they always have an excuse? Do they talk about how everyone else is the problem, but never look at their own contribution?

Watch how they treat people who can't do anything for them. How do they talk to the receptionist? What do they say about colleagues who aren't in the room? When they make a mistake, do they own it or deflect?

If someone consistently shows you they're not reliable, believe them. If drama follows them from project to project, that's not bad luck, that's a pattern. If they're always the victim in every story they tell, pay attention to that.

And document your work on shared projects. Keep emails showing what you delivered and when. If you raise a concern about something, put it in writing. Not in an aggressive way, just a simple "Following up on our conversation, here's my understanding..."

Because if things go sideways later, you want a clear record of what you actually said and did.

If you sense a project is heading in a questionable direction, or someone you're working with is making choices you can't stand behind, create some distance. You don't have to make it dramatic. You can be busy with other priorities. You can respectfully decline the next collaboration. You can redirect your energy to projects with people whose judgment you trust.

I know this might feel like you're being calculating or not giving people a chance. But when you protect your reputation, you're protecting your personal brand in the same way a company would. That's being realistic not mean.

If your reputation gets damaged by association, you lose your ability to influence anything. You can't mentor people. You can't get picked for the projects you care about. You can't build the kind of career that actually lets you make the changes you want to see.

Your reputation amplifies everything else you bring to the table. When people trust you, your ideas land better. Your recommendations carry weight. People want to work with you. But when there's a question mark next to your name, even if it's not fair, even if it's just guilt by association, everything gets harder.

Before you say yes to a collaboration, a committee, a project team? Do a little homework. Ask around about the other people involved. Look at their track record. Watch how they handle pressure and conflict.

Your name matters. Be intentional about who gets to stand next to it on the letterhead.

Because rebuilding a reputation? That takes way more energy than protecting it would have taken in the first place.

27

LEAD WITH VISION,
NOT JUST LOGIC

Since we talked about reading your environment and adapting your style, I keep thinking about what actually moves people once you've learned to speak their language.

And here's what nobody tells you: logic convinces the head, but vision captures the heart. And once people's hearts are engaged, they'll follow you places logic could never take them.

I watched this play out during a massive company restructuring. Everyone was terrified. Layoffs, uncertainty, chaos. An IT executive was leading one of the teams through it.

She could have gone the typical route. Shown them the spreadsheets, explained the rationale, made it all make sense logically. That would have gotten compliance.

Instead, she painted a picture. "We're not just surviving this merger," she told them. "We're going to be the team that shows this entire company what excellence looks like. In six months, they're going to be studying how we handled this transition."

Was it risky? Absolutely. But something magical happened. Her team stopped acting like victims of change and started acting like pioneers of it.

They worked harder, collaborated better, and made Melissa's vision come true. Same situation, same people. But vision transformed everything logic couldn't touch.

This builds perfectly on reading your environment. When you can inspire belief in your vision, you're not just adapting to power dynamics. You're actively shaping how people see the future.

Think about Steve Jobs. Apple doesn't sell you a phone by listing processor speeds. They sell you the belief that you're "thinking different." It's not about the product. It's about the identity you get to claim when you buy it.

But when men speak with sweeping conviction, they're called visionary leaders. When we do it, we're often labeled as dramatic or emotional. So many of us learned to stick to the facts, hoping our logic would be enough.

It's not enough.

The answer isn't to abandon logic. It's to lead with vision and back it with facts. Start with where you're going and why it matters, then show them how you'll get there. Vision opens the door, logic seals the deal.

In your next presentation, try starting differently. Instead of diving into data, begin with the destination. "When we finish this project, we'll have created something that changes how this entire industry thinks about customer service." Then show them the numbers.

Same work, completely different energy in the room.

I'm not talking about manipulation or creating false hope. Vision with integrity is about aligning people around something meaningful and then delivering on it.

Look at how Mary Barra transformed General Motors. She didn't just focus on quarterly earnings. She gave the company a bigger story: zero crashes, zero emissions, zero congestion. People rallied around that purpose in ways they never would have for profit margins alone.

Your expertise gets you in the room. Your vision gets people to follow you out of it.

Stop waiting for permission to be inspiring. Stop hiding behind data because it feels safer than stating what you believe.

Lead with where you're going, why it matters, and who you're becoming in the process.

Because the world has enough people who can prove what's wrong. What we need are more people who can paint a picture of what's possible.

28

STOP WAITING TO FEEL READY

Okay, I need to talk about something that's been making me absolutely furious.

You're sitting there with the perfect idea, the right answer, the solution everyone needs. But you're waiting. Waiting to think it through one more time. Waiting to make sure it's perfect. Waiting for the ideal opening.

And then someone else speaks up. Someone with a half-baked version of your brilliant idea. And suddenly they're the one getting credit, getting noticed, getting asked to lead the follow-up.

And I want to scream because this keeps happening and we keep letting it happen.

The world doesn't reward the most prepared person. It rewards the person who moves first with enough confidence to make others believe in their direction.

I learned this watching a crisis meeting. Our biggest partner was threatening to leave, and the room was full of senior people scrambling for solutions. I had spent the weekend analyzing their complaints. I had a solid recovery plan.

But I wanted to polish it more. Make sure every detail was perfect. Wait for the right moment when I could present it flawlessly.

Meanwhile, another woman stood up and said, "Here's what we're going to do." Her plan wasn't as thorough as mine. It had gaps I could see from across the room.

But she delivered it with such conviction that the entire energy shifted. Within five minutes, she was leading the response team.

My better plan? Never saw the light of day because I'd hesitated too long.

And I'm so tired of this. Tired of watching women wait for perfect conditions while men move forward with 60% readiness and figure out the rest as they go.

Studies literally show this. Men apply for jobs when they meet 60% of the qualifications. Women wait until they meet 100%. Same opportunity, completely different willingness to be bold before being "ready."

Perfect conditions don't exist. There will always be something you could prepare more, someone who might have more experience, a reason to wait just a little longer.

But boldness has its own power. When you act decisively, people assume you know something they don't. Your confidence becomes contagious.

So what does boldness actually look like?

Speak up in meetings even when your idea isn't fully formed. A good idea shared beats a perfect idea kept silent.

Apply for positions you're 70% qualified for instead of waiting until you meet every requirement.

Pitch yourself for opportunities instead of hoping someone will notice you deserve them.

Make decisions quickly when you have enough information, rather than endlessly researching every possible angle.

I'm not talking about reckless action. Bold doesn't mean thoughtless. It means being willing to move forward with imperfect information because you understand that timing matters as much as preparation.

Stop doing that to yourself. Stop waiting for perfect timing that never comes. Stop letting less qualified people take opportunities you were overqualified for, simply because they had the audacity to move when you were still preparing.

Move boldly. The world is waiting for what you have to offer, but it won't wait forever.

29

MAP BACKWARDS FROM
WHAT YOU WANT

Something's been nagging at me since we talked about moving with boldness and leading with vision. I keep thinking about how many incredibly capable women I know who can paint beautiful pictures of the future but somehow never quite get there.

They're always hustling, always busy, always putting out fires. But ask them where they'll be in two years, and they get this deer-in-headlights look.

Vision without a roadmap is just wishful thinking.

I know a woman who has this amazing dream of opening her own marketing agency. She talks about it constantly, has all these ideas about the kind of campaigns she'd create, the brands she'd work with. But when I asked her what concrete steps she was taking to get there, she went blank.

"I'm working on building my skills," she said. "Getting more experience."

That's not a plan. That's just existing.

Meanwhile, another woman I know wanted something similar. But she started from the end and worked backward. She wanted to be fully independent in three years. So she mapped it out: Year one, build a client base while working part-time. Year two, transition to full-time with three anchor clients. Year three, scale to her target revenue.

Then she worked backward from each milestone. To have three anchor clients by year two, she needed to start those conversations in month six of year one. To do that, she needed specific expertise they'd value, which meant taking on particular projects in her current job.

Guess who's running her own agency now?

This connects to everything we've talked about. Remember when we discussed concentrating your forces? The most important force to concentrate is your future. When you own the outcome you want, every decision becomes easier because you know whether it moves you toward that ending or away from it.

Think about how Taylor Swift handled losing control of her master recordings. She could have wallowed in victimhood or accepted that someone else would always control her work. Instead, she mapped backwards from the outcome she wanted: total ownership of her music.

What would make that possible? Re-recording everything. What would make re-recording successful? Fan support and media attention. How do you get that? By making it a crusade for artist rights, not just a personal grudge.

She didn't just react to what happened to her. She designed what would happen next.

But most people mess this up. They think planning means predicting everything perfectly. That's impossible and exhausting. Real planning means knowing your destination and having backup routes when the main road gets blocked.

I learned this the hard way when I was trying to make a major career transition. I had this beautiful five-year plan, perfectly mapped out. Then the economy crashed, my industry shifted, and half my plan became obsolete.

For about two weeks, I felt like a complete failure. Then I realized something: my destination hadn't changed, just the route. So I mapped new paths to the same outcome. Some detours ended up being better than my original plan.

That's what owning the outcome really means. Not controlling every variable, but staying focused on where you're going no matter what obstacles appear.

Women especially need this skill because we're constantly praised for being great at execution. "She's so reliable." "She always delivers." "She handles whatever you throw at her."

All of that sounds positive, right? But execution without strategy keeps you trapped. You become the person who makes other people's visions happen instead of the person with the vision.

Men are celebrated for being visionaries even when their execution is sloppy. Women are expected to execute flawlessly while someone else gets to be the visionary. That dynamic keeps us in supporting roles no matter how talented we are.

The next time someone offers you a new opportunity, don't just ask "Can I do this well?" Ask "Where does this lead me?" If it doesn't connect to an outcome you actually want, it's just busy work dressed up as opportunity.

Pick something you genuinely want to achieve in the next two to three years. Not what you think you should want, but something that actually excites you when you imagine it. I'm willing to bet you already know what it is. You've just been too busy executing everyone else's plans to map your own.

What needs to be true six months before that outcome happens? A year before? Two years before? Work backward and map the milestones. Not in some elaborate business plan format, just clarity about what needs to happen when.

Then start making decisions based on whether they move you toward your mapped destination. Say no to opportunities that don't align, even if they seem impressive on paper. This is where everything we've talked about comes together. You're not just saying no to protect your energy, you're saying no because you have somewhere specific you're going.

This is where all our previous discussions converge. When you've learned to read people, you can identify who will help you reach your outcome. When you've mastered strategic surrender, you know which battles don't serve your endgame. When you move with boldness, you're moving toward something specific, not just moving for the sake of motion.

But without this, without knowing where you're actually going, all those skills just make you a more effective person going nowhere in particular.

The women who last, who build something meaningful, who create change that outlives them? They all understand this. They're not just good at their jobs. They're architects of their own futures.

They don't wait to see what opportunities come their way. They create a destination and then reverse-engineer the path to get there.

Stop letting life happen to you. Start designing what happens next.

Because the difference between women who dream and women who achieve isn't talent or luck. It's the ability to map backwards from what they want and then execute that map with relentless focus.

Your future is too important to leave to chance. Own it.

MAKE IT LOOK EASY, GET PAID LIKE IT'S HARD

So there's this thing that keeps happening to me, and I only recently figured out what was going on.

I'm really good at presentations. Like, genuinely good. I can walk into a room, read the energy, adapt on the fly, handle tough questions, and make it all look smooth and effortless.

For years, I thought this was an advantage. Look how naturally this comes to me! Look how easy I make it look!

Then I noticed something weird. When compensation reviews came around, I wasn't getting paid like someone with a rare, valuable skill. I was getting paid like someone doing routine work that just happened to be pleasant.

My manager would say things like, "Well, you're just naturally good with people. This is easy for you."

Easy. As if I hadn't spent fifteen years learning how to read rooms, manage personalities, and navigate difficult conversations. As if "being good with people" wasn't a skill I'd deliberately developed and refined.

Meanwhile, my colleague who was "good with data" got promoted twice in the same period. Nobody told him his analytical skills were just "natural."

I started paying attention to this pattern. The smoother I made things look, the less people valued the work behind them.

When I delivered a flawless presentation, people assumed it was no big deal. When I defused a tense project situation, they figured I just had a knack for it. When I solved a complex problem elegantly, they thought the problem must not have been that complex.

My effortlessness was actually working against me.

But I also noticed: the women who succeeded weren't the ones making everything look difficult. That just made them look incompetent.

The successful ones made strategic things look effortless while making sure key people understood the difficulty behind the smoothness.

So I started experimenting. After I delivered a smooth presentation, I'd follow up with my manager privately. Not complaining, just educating.

"I'm glad the Johnson presentation went well. I want you to know I spent twelve hours researching their industry challenges and built three different approaches based on their potential concerns. The fact that it looked smooth meant the preparation paid off."

Same effortless delivery in public. But now my manager understood that smooth wasn't the same as easy.

Within two review cycles, my compensation jumped significantly. Same skills. Same results. Different awareness of the value behind them.

I also started documenting my preparation process. Not to brag, but to have evidence when it mattered.

Don't just say you're good at something, show it with evidence. Start keeping track of your work and preparation process. Not for show, but so you have real data to back you up when opportunities come around.

When it's time to make your case, move from vague claims to concrete proof. Instead of saying, "I'm great at client relationships," say something like, "This year I gave 23 presentations with a 94% close rate. Each one took about 15 hours of prep. That's 345 hours of work that brought in $3.2 million in new business."

Numbers turn talent into expertise. Evidence turns perception into credibility. The lesson? Effortlessness is powerful when you use it strategically. But you have to make sure decision-makers understand that effortless doesn't mean easy or free.

Your effortlessness should create mystique and admiration. Your strategy should turn that into advancement and appropriate compensation.

Master both, and you're not just admired. You're indispensable and properly valued.

31

GIVE THEM CHOICES
YOU CAN LIVE WITH

I watched a colleague get boxed into a corner last week. Her manager called her into his office and laid out two options: take on a massive project with no additional support, or he'd interpret her hesitation as "not being ready for the next level."

She took the project. Then spent the next three months drowning while he got credit for "developing talent."

That's what happens when someone else is dealing the cards.

Women get these false choice scenarios constantly. "Either prove you can handle everything we throw at you, or admit you're not leadership material." "Either be accommodating or be labeled difficult." "Either sacrifice work-life balance or accept you're not serious about your career."

Men rarely face these binary traps because they're already assumed to be leadership material. They get asked "How can we support you in taking on this challenge?" while we get asked "Are you sure you can handle this?"

Here's what most people miss about influence: real power isn't about being the best at playing whatever hand you're dealt. It's about being the person who shuffles the deck.

I learned this from watching a woman named Camila navigate what looked like an impossible situation. Her company wanted her to relocate to a struggling office to "turn it around." It was a classic setup for failure. She could say yes and risk her reputation on a potentially unsalvageable situation, or say no and be seen as "not committed."

Instead, she reframed it entirely. "I'm excited about the turnaround challenge. I see two paths that could work: I could relocate and lead it full-time with a VP title and expanded budget, or I could stay here and advise remotely while we bring in someone local to execute. Both could succeed, but they require different resources."

Suddenly, she wasn't the one being tested. She was the strategist offering solutions. She ended up getting the VP title, choosing to relocate on her terms, and actually succeeding because she'd negotiated the support she needed.

That's the power of controlling the options.

Listen...instead of asking open-ended questions that put you at someone else's mercy, frame the choices. Instead of "What do you want me to prioritize?" try "I can focus on either the retention strategy or the new product launch this quarter. Which would create more value for the team?"

Notice what just happened? You shifted from order-taker to strategist. They're still making the decision, but you controlled what they could decide between.

This works in negotiations too. When someone presents a lowball salary, don't just argue about their number. Structure options instead. "I'm flexible on how we approach compensation. We could do a base salary of X with performance bonuses, or a higher base of Y with expanded responsibilities. What fits better with your budget planning?"

You can protect your boundaries with it too. When someone dumps an "urgent" request on you, frame the reality. "I can give you a quick analysis by tomorrow, or a thorough report by Thursday. Which timeline works better for your decision?"

The key is making sure your options are genuinely viable. If people sense manipulation, this backfires spectacularly. You want them feeling guided, not trapped.

Most people actually prefer having options presented to them. It feels helpful, not controlling. It takes cognitive load off them and positions you as someone who thinks strategically.

But here's where the line is: this only works when you genuinely care about finding solutions that work for everyone. The moment it becomes purely self-serving, people will sense it and shut you out.

Notice how this changes your reputation over time. You become the person who thinks strategically, who brings clarity when others see chaos, who navigates tricky situations and finds paths forward. You're not the person who says no. You're the person who finds ways to yes.

Think about the last time someone presented you with a binary choice that felt like a trap. What if you'd reframed it with two options you could actually live with? How might that have changed the dynamic?

The goal isn't to control every conversation. It's to stop being at the mercy of other people's limited thinking about what's possible.

When you shape the choices, you shape the outcome. And that's not manipulation. That's leadership.

Stop accepting false binaries designed to pressure you into bad decisions. Start presenting real options that serve everyone's interests, including yours.

Because the woman who controls the options doesn't just influence the decision. She changes the entire nature of the conversation.

32

CREATE THE CLUB EVERYONE WANTS TO JOIN

Here's a quick case study. A masterclass for how to make people want to be part of something bigger. Sophia runs a small marketing agency. Six employees, decent client list, nothing flashy. But here's what's interesting: she gets about fifty applications every time she posts a job opening. Not because she pays more than competitors. Not because she offers better benefits.

It's because people want to work for her. They want to be able to say "I work at Sophia's agency."

She created something people want to be part of.

Here's the bottom line: People don't just want good work, good products, or good leadership. They want to belong to something that makes them feel special, chosen, part of an inner circle.

And honey, this is where women actually have a secret advantage if we're willing to use it. We've been building communities and creating belonging forever. It's just that nobody told us this skill translates directly to power and influence in professional settings.

Men often build hierarchies. Women often build networks. Both have value, but belonging, the kind that makes people genuinely want to be part of what you're building? That's our territory if we claim it.

Listen, stop thinking only about what you're offering and start thinking about the identity you're creating. What does it mean to be part of your team, your project, your vision? What does it say about someone that they're associated with you?

Sophia's agency has this thing where they only take on clients they believe in. Sounds simple, but it creates this sense among her team that they're doing work that matters. They're not just marketers. They're the marketers who have standards. That identity is powerful.

And she's deliberate about the language she uses. Notice how the best leaders use "we" and "us" rather than "me" and "them." "We're the kind of people who..." creates instant tribal identity.

When someone on Sophia's team talks about a project, they say "We only work with companies trying to make a real difference." That "we" includes them in something bigger than a job. It makes them feel chosen.

Here's what makes people want to be part of something: the feeling that they're on the inside of something special. Not exclusive in a snobby way, but exclusive in a "we get it and they don't" way. People crave that feeling of being part of a group that sees what others miss.

One of my colleagues does this brilliantly with her department. She'll say things like "You know how our team operates differently than other departments? That's because we actually trust each other to get things done." She's creating an identity: we're the department that works smarter because we're better at collaboration.

Sophia's team has inside jokes, a shared Spotify playlist for the office, a tradition of Friday afternoon project retrospectives where they celebrate wins and learn from mistakes. Small things that signal "you're part of this." These aren't just activities, they're proof that you belong to something special.

And she's smart about how she talks about people who aren't in the "club." Not in a mean way, but in a way that highlights what makes her group different. "Other agencies might do it that way, but we value authentic relationships with our clients over just closing deals."

When someone joins her team, she makes entry feel meaningful. New hires spend their first week shadowing different team members, learning not just the work but "how we do things here." By the end of that week, they feel like they've been initiated into something real.

But here's the critical part, and this is where a lot of people mess this up: the "club" has to deliver on what it promises. If you create an identity around excellence but accept mediocrity, people will see through it. If you talk about values but don't live them, your "club" becomes a joke.

The belonging has to be real. People want to be part of something that actually means something, not just clever branding.

I've seen women build extraordinary cultures this way: teams where people genuinely support each other, where collaboration isn't just a buzzword, where people stay not because they have to but because they want to. Meanwhile, I've watched male-led teams with higher salaries hemorrhage talent because nobody felt like they belonged to anything meaningful.

That's not an accident. Women often understand instinctively that people don't just work for paychecks. They work for purpose, for belonging, for the feeling that they're part of something that matters.

Think about what your work, your team, your projects actually stand for. What would make someone proud to say they're associated with you? What identity are you offering them? Not the polished mission statement, the real culture underneath.

Where could you create more sense of "we" in how you communicate? What rituals or symbols could reinforce belonging? These don't have to be elaborate, sometimes the smallest traditions create the strongest sense of community.

The question to ask yourself when you're building a team or launching a project is this: "Would people want to be part of this even if there wasn't a paycheck attached?" If the answer is yes, you've created something powerful.

Because people don't just follow competence. They follow belonging. They want to be part of the club that sees what others miss, that does what others won't, that stands for something others don't.

Give them that club, and they'll not only join, they'll recruit others for you.

And that's how you build influence that doesn't depend on your title or your budget. You build it through creating something people genuinely want to be part of.

33

STOP HANDING PEOPLE YOUR WEAK SPOTS

Let me tell you about the moment I realized someone was using my own weakness against me.

I was working with this manager who had figured out that I craved recognition. Every time he needed someone to work late or take on an impossible deadline, he'd start with the flattery. "You're the only one I trust with something this important." "The division chief specifically asked for you because you're so reliable."

It felt amazing. Until I realized my colleagues weren't getting the same requests. They were going home at reasonable hours while I was burning myself out for praise that cost him nothing to give.

That's what happens when you don't guard your pressure points. Someone figures out what makes you tick and uses it like a remote control.

Let me be clear: women are especially vulnerable to this because we've been socialized to respond to specific triggers. Need approval? We've been taught that being liked matters more than being respected. Fear of disappointing people? We've been raised to be accommodating.

Desire to be seen as helpful? That's been our currency for acceptance since childhood.

Men manipulate these buttons constantly, often without even realizing they're doing it, because they know women are conditioned to respond.

The reality is, there are people who study others for weaknesses the way predators study prey. They notice who needs approval and overwork them with compliments. They see who avoids conflict and steamroll them with aggressive tactics. They spot financial anxiety and use it to underpay or control.

You don't need to become one of those people. But you absolutely need to recognize when someone's doing it to you.

Listen, the first step is identifying your own triggers. What do people use to get you to say yes when you want to say no? Fear of disappointing someone? Need for approval? Desire to be seen as helpful? Worry about job security?

I had to sit down and actually write mine out. It was uncomfortable, but necessary. My big one was needing to be seen as competent, which meant I'd take on anything to prove I could handle it, even when it was setting me up for failure.

Once you know your triggers, watch for the patterns. Pay attention to who asks what of you and how they frame it. Do certain people only reach out when they need something? Do they use specific language that hits your emotional buttons?

I had a colleague who would always start requests with "I know this is a lot to ask, but you're the only one who can do this right..." She knew my competence trigger and played it like a violin.

Here's a practical move that saved me: practice the pause. When someone makes a request that triggers your people-pleasing instincts, don't answer immediately. Say, "Let me check my capacity and get back to you." That tiny delay can save you from making decisions based on manipulation instead of logic.

My friend Ramona learned this after becoming the office "fixer," the person everyone dumped their problems on because she always found solutions. She loved feeling needed until she realized she was drowning while everyone else stayed dry.

Her defensive move? She started saying, "I can help with this crisis, but I'll need additional support for next time." Suddenly she wasn't just the go-to problem solver. She was the strategic thinker who came with conditions.

And here's what's interesting: when she stopped being the easy yes, people respected her more, not less. Because she was no longer the pushover. She was the expert who had boundaries.

You also need to know your own leverage. Where are you already indispensable? What skills, relationships, or knowledge make others depend on you? Don't let that stay invisible. Document it. Highlight it. Make sure the right people know about it.

But here's the tricky part: being indispensable can make you a target. If you're the only person holding something critical together, some people will try to weaken or replace you. So you want to be valuable in ways that are hard to duplicate while staying adaptable enough to pivot.

Think about it this way: you've got vulnerabilities, places where you're easy to manipulate. And you've got strengths, places where others need you. The question is how you protect the first while leveraging the second.

For me, I had to stop responding to flattery as if it were payment. I had to recognize when someone was playing my need for approval instead of actually valuing my work. And I had to get comfortable with the discomfort of disappointing people who were trying to exploit my people-pleasing tendencies.

The goal isn't to become cold or calculating. It's to stop being the easy target for someone else's manipulation.

When you guard your pressure points, you don't just protect yourself from exploitation. You earn respect. People can't corner you as easily, so they have to engage with you as an equal instead of trying to control you through your weaknesses.

Stop handing people the instruction manual for how to manipulate you. Stop making yourself the easy yes. Stop proving your worth by saying yes to things that diminish you.

You get to keep your kindness, your helpfulness, your desire to do good work. You just get to do it on your terms instead of someone else's.

34

WALK IN LIKE YOU OWN THE ROOM

I have to tell you about this moment that changed everything for me. I was sitting in a boardroom full of executives, and I noticed something that made my stomach drop. The two other women in the room were both hunched over, taking notes, barely making eye contact. Meanwhile, every man was leaning back in his chair like he owned the place.

And then it hit me: people treat you exactly how you signal they should.

If you walk into a room apologizing for your presence, shrinking into corners, waiting for permission to speak, that's how they'll treat you. Like you're grateful just to be there.

But if you carry yourself like you belong? Everything changes.

And honey, I know this might sound superficial, but your body language is having a conversation before you even open your mouth. And right now, what is your posture saying about you?

Here's what drives me crazy: women are socialized to make ourselves smaller. Literally smaller. Don't take up too much space. Don't be too loud. Don't seem too confident or you'll be labeled arrogant. Meanwhile, men are taught that confidence, even unfounded confidence, is attractive. They're rewarded for swagger.

We get punished for the exact same behavior that gets them promoted.

Listen, before you walk into any important space, take thirty seconds to reset your entire presence. Pull your shoulders back. Ground your feet. Make your voice slightly slower than nerves want it to be. Take up the space you're entitled to instead of trying to disappear.

I watched my friend Naomi transform her entire career by making this one shift. She had the expertise, the track record, everything. But she was getting passed over repeatedly because she carried herself like she was apologizing for being smart.

Her coach made her practice walking into rooms like she owned them. Not arrogant, just certain. Within six months, she was being invited to strategy meetings she'd never been included in before.

Nothing about her skills changed. Everything about how people perceived those skills did.

This isn't about fake confidence or pretending to be someone you're not. It's about alignment. Your presence should match the value you bring. Your posture should reflect the respect you deserve.

That's what commanding presence looks like. Not demanding attention through dramatics, but commanding respect through certainty.

And here's the part that might surprise you: this works even when you're learning, even when you're new, even when you feel like you have no idea what you're doing.

Confidence means trusting that you can figure it out when you don't know everything.

Here's something I learned the hard way: when someone challenges you or questions your authority, don't rush to over-explain or justify yourself. Pause. Take a breath. Answer directly and then stop talking.

People who own the room don't scramble to prove themselves. They respond and move on.

I used to word-vomit when challenged, throwing out every credential and justification I could think of. Know what that communicated? That I wasn't sure I deserved to be there. Once I learned to just answer the question and move on, the challenges decreased dramatically.

But let me be clear about something, this isn't about becoming cold or unapproachable. You can be warm and gracious while still maintaining your authority. You can be collaborative while still claiming your space.

The difference is in your baseline energy. Instead of starting from a place of "I hope you'll accept me," you start from "I'm here to contribute something valuable."

That shift changes everything. How people listen to you. How they respond to your ideas. Whether they interrupt you or wait for you to finish.

Your presence is your first negotiation. Make sure you're winning it.

Next time you're in a group conversation, notice your physical position. Are you leaning in desperately, trying to find a way into the discussion? Or are you grounded, speaking when you have something to add, comfortable with silence?

The reality is, you're going to be scrutinized more than your male colleagues. That's not paranoia, that's fact. People are watching how you dress, how you speak, how you react under pressure.

When a man shows up to a meeting in jeans and a t-shirt, he's "casual and approachable." When we do it, we're "not taking things seriously." He can interrupt and he's "passionate." We interrupt and we're "aggressive."

The rules are different. It's exhausting and it's not fair. But that also means when you get your presence right, the impact is enormous. When you walk into a room grounded and intentional, you disarm critics before they even open their mouths.

Think about where you need to show up differently. That meeting where you always defer. That conference where you hang back instead of introducing yourself. That presentation where you rush through your points because you're afraid of taking up too much time.

What would change if you walked in like you owned the room? I'm willing to bet you already know the answer. You've just been too conditioned to apologize for your presence to claim it.

Not because you're entitled. Not because you're better than anyone else. But because you've earned your place there and you're done apologizing for it.

Stand like you belong everywhere you go. Because honestly? You do.

Stop shrinking. Stop apologizing with your body language for having expertise. Stop waiting for permission to take up space you've already earned.

Walk in like you own the room. Because the alternative is walking in like you're lucky to be allowed in it.

TIMING BEATS TALENT
EVERY TIME

I need to tell you about the most talented woman I ever worked with. Brilliant strategist. Creative problem solver. Could see around corners that others didn't even know existed.

She should have been running the company by now. Instead, she's stuck in middle management, watching less talented people get promoted around her.

What happened? Her timing was terrible.

She'd push for changes when leadership wasn't ready to hear them. She'd launch initiatives right before budget freezes. She'd make bold moves during periods when the company needed stability. Her ideas were good, often great. But she kept trying to plant seeds in winter and wondering why nothing grew.

Meanwhile, another colleague with half her strategic vision kept getting promoted. Not because his ideas were better, but because he had this uncanny ability to sense when leadership was ready to hear something. He'd wait for the right moment, when conditions were favorable, when the right people were paying attention, when the organization had capacity to actually implement changes.

His mediocre ideas at perfect timing beat her brilliant ideas at terrible timing every single time.

That's what I need you to understand. Timing isn't just about being patient. It's about reading the moment and knowing when to move and when to wait.

Think about how great investors make money. They don't just pick good companies. They pick good companies at the right time. Buy too early and you lose money waiting. Buy too late and you miss the opportunity. The skill is knowing when the conditions are right.

Or look at how successful product launches work. The iPhone wasn't successful just because it was innovative. Apple launched it at the perfect moment when technology had advanced enough to support the vision, when consumer behavior was ready to shift, when the market was hungry for something new.

Timing amplified everything else.

But women aren't usually taught to think strategically about timing. We're taught to work hard, be prepared, and speak up. All good advice. But incomplete.

Because working hard at the wrong time just means you work hard for nothing. Being prepared for a conversation that's happening too early or too late means your preparation doesn't matter. Speaking up when no one's ready to hear you means you've burned credibility for no gain.

I learned this watching how major organizational changes actually happen. There's always this period before a change where leadership is frustrated with the current state but not yet ready to act. Then there's a window where they're actively looking for solutions. Then there's a period after they've made decisions where new input just feels like criticism.

If you pitch your idea during that first phase, you're too early. They'll thank you for your thoughts and nothing will happen. If you pitch during the third phase, you're too late. They've already committed to a different direction.

But if you pitch during that middle window, when they're actively seeking solutions? Your idea gets implemented even if it's not dramatically better than what you suggested six months earlier.

Same idea. Different timing. Completely different outcome.

So how do you actually develop this timing sense? You watch for patterns in how decisions get made. When does leadership typically approve new initiatives? What conditions need to be present? What signals indicate they're open to change versus locked into current direction?

You read organizational mood. Is the company in growth mode or survival mode? Are people feeling confident or anxious? Is leadership focused on innovation or stability? Your pitch needs to match the mood.

You pay attention to personal timing. Is your manager dealing with a crisis right now? Did they just get great news or bad news? Are they under pressure from their own boss? All of this affects whether they can even hear what you're saying.

And you build patience. Just because you've figured something out doesn't mean everyone else is ready to hear it. Sometimes the smartest move is sitting on a brilliant idea until conditions ripen.

I had a manager who wanted to propose a major process change. She'd identified the problem, developed a solution, and was ready to pitch. But when we looked at timing, we realized her group had just gone through two major transitions. Leadership was exhausted from change. The organization needed stability, not another initiative.

We waited four months. Let things settle. Let leadership catch their breath. Then, when they started looking forward again instead of backward, she pitched her idea. It was approved immediately and she got to lead the implementation.

If she'd pushed when she first wanted to, she would have been told "not now" and her idea would have been dead. Patience turned a good idea into a career-defining project.

Think about something you've been trying to push forward that isn't gaining traction. Is the problem really your idea, or is it your timing? Are you trying to plant in winter?

What would change if you waited for the right season? Not forever, just until conditions were favorable.

The next time you have an idea you're excited about, don't automatically rush to pitch it. Ask yourself: Is this the right moment? Are the people I need to influence ready to hear this? What conditions would need to exist for this idea to land well?

Then watch for those conditions. Build your case while you're waiting. Refine your pitch. Gather supporting evidence. So when the moment arrives, you're ready to move decisively.

Because the woman who moves first with a mediocre idea at perfect timing will beat the woman who has a brilliant idea at terrible timing every single time.

Stop pushing against closed doors. Start watching for the moment when those doors begin to open.

Your talent matters. Your preparation matters. But timing? That's what turns potential into results.

36

BUILD YOUR OWN DAMN DOOR

Okay, we need to have a direct conversation about something you're doing that's quietly killing your career.

You're waiting.

Waiting for your boss to notice your potential. Waiting for someone to tap you on the shoulder and say "you're ready." Waiting for permission to do the thing you already know needs doing.

Meanwhile, someone with half your qualifications just did it without asking and is getting praised for their initiative.

Women hands down do this more than men because we've been socialized to wait for permission. To be chosen. To prove we're worthy of being included. Meanwhile, the Jacks, Johns, and Davids of the world are out there building their own opportunities without asking anyone if they deserve them.

We're taught that if we just work hard enough, prove ourselves enough, wait patiently enough, someone will finally recognize our worth and give us what we deserve. That's a trap. Because you're giving someone else control over your trajectory while you sit there hoping they'll notice you.

There's this woman who works at a busy restaurant. For months, she kept asking the manager to train her on the specialty cocktail station. It was the highest-tip position, and she knew she'd be amazing at it. But week after week, he'd give those shifts to other people while she stayed stuck taking food orders.

She could have kept pushing, kept asking, kept making herself smaller by begging for scraps. Instead, she decided to starve that distraction. She started learning wine service on her own time and building relationships with the sommelier at the wine bar next door. Within two months, they offered her a position that paid better than the cocktail station ever would have.

Stop chasing what someone won't give you. Start building what they can't take away.

You know this feeling, right? Maybe it was that friend group that never quite included you. Maybe it's the collaboration opportunity that keeps going to someone else. Maybe it's your ex who moved on while you're still analyzing what went wrong.

Every minute you spend fixated on what you don't have is a minute you're not investing in what you could create.

There's a teacher who spent two years trying to get assigned to the advanced placement classes. She had the credentials, the passion, the track record. But the department head kept giving those plum assignments to his favorites. She was burning herself out trying to prove she deserved what was never going to be offered.

Finally, she stopped. Instead of fighting for his approval, she started an after-school college prep program. Word spread. Parents requested her specifically. Within a year, colleges were reaching out to her for student recommendations, and her program became more prestigious than the official AP classes ever were.

She stopped begging to be let in. She built her own damn door.

A freelance designer kept chasing these ideal clients who never seemed to commit. They'd string her along with "maybe next quarter" and "we're still deciding." Meanwhile, she was turning down smaller projects to keep her schedule open for them.

When she finally stopped waiting for their approval and started showcasing her work on social media, better clients found her. Ones who didn't need convincing. Ones who valued what she brought.

Here's the difference between giving up and strategically redirecting: Giving up feels defeated. Strategic redirection feels powerful because you're choosing where to put your focus instead of letting someone else control it.

You don't do any of this out of spite or manipulation. You do it because your energy is precious, and you're going to invest it where it actually grows.

Think about three things you've been wanting that aren't happening. Maybe it's a work opportunity, a relationship situation, or a social acceptance issue. Look at each one honestly and ask yourself: Is this actually serving me, or is it just a distraction that's keeping me from building something better?

I'm willing to bet at least one of those things is pure distraction, an energy drain you need to starve starting today.

A nursing student kept trying to get into this exclusive study group that never invited her. She'd hint about it, try to prove her worth, even offer to bring snacks. Meanwhile, she was neglecting her own study routine. When she finally stopped caring about their group and focused on her own preparation, her grades improved so much that other students started asking her for help.

Sometimes the thing you think you need is actually keeping you from the thing you're meant to build.

Here's the psychological edge that comes with this: when you stop chasing, people notice. There's something deeply unsettling about someone who refuses to beg for what they want. It shifts the entire dynamic.

The manager who was withholding the promotion suddenly wonders why you stopped asking about it. The friend who was taking your attention for granted gets confused when you're not as available. The client who was stringing you along realizes they might actually lose you.

That's not manipulation. That's natural human psychology. We want what seems scarce or unavailable.

But here's the most important part: you can't fake this. You can't pretend not to care while secretly obsessing. You have to actually redirect your energy into something that genuinely excites you more than whatever you were chasing.

I learned this when I spent months trying to get included in a strategic planning committee that kept filling seats with the same insiders. I pitched ideas, volunteered for extra work, and made myself visible.

Nothing. They just weren't interested in what I brought to the table.

So I stopped trying. I started my own cross-departmental initiative instead. Within six months, leadership was asking me to present my work at company-wide meetings. The committee I'd been desperate to join? Suddenly irrelevant.

When you starve the distraction, you don't just protect your energy. You discover what you're actually capable of when you're not pouring yourself into someone else's maybe.

Stop waiting to be chosen. Stop proving you're worthy of opportunities that should be chasing you. Stop making yourself smaller trying to fit through doors that were never meant to open for you.

Not every door is meant for you. Not every opportunity deserves your chase. Sometimes the most powerful thing you can do is shrug, turn around, and build your own entrance.

Because the woman who builds her own door? She doesn't need anyone's permission to walk through it.

37

STAND OUT OR STAY STUCK

Last week I watched something that made my blood boil. A colleague of mine, a brilliant woman who works her ass off, spent three weeks on a comprehensive analysis. I'm talking spreadsheets, competitive research, the whole nine yards. She presented it in a meeting, and I watched everyone's eyes glaze over halfway through.

Then this guy, mediocre at best, makes one snarky comment about "disrupting the market" and suddenly everyone's leaning forward, nodding like he just invented fire.

Two days later, guess whose name came up when leadership was talking about "innovative thinkers"? Not hers.

I know you've lived this exact scenario. You've done the work, delivered the results, showed up prepared, and somehow it's like you're invisible while someone else gets the credit for being "memorable."

Here's what nobody tells you: people don't remember everything you do. They remember the moments that cut through the noise.

In a world where attention spans are shrinking and everyone's scrolling past everything, power belongs to the woman who creates moments that stick. Not by being the loudest person in the room, but by being the most memorable.

And listen, women are often told to be "professional," which somehow gets translated to "forgettable." We're encouraged to be thorough, detailed, and comprehensive. All of which are important, but none of which are memorable if that's all we bring.

Meanwhile, men throw out half-baked ideas with supreme confidence and get remembered for "thinking big." We do the actual work and get forgotten for "not having executive presence."

There's a quality control supervisor at a manufacturing plant who was getting frustrated because her safety recommendations kept getting ignored. She'd submit detailed reports about potential hazards, but management would skim through them and move on to other priorities.

So she tried something different. Instead of starting her next safety meeting with statistics, she brought in a single work boot with a steel toe that had been crushed in an accident. She set it on the conference table and said, "This boot saved someone's foot last week. Now let me show you the five places where the next one might not."

The room went completely still. Every manager leaned forward to look. She had their full attention before she even pulled out her data.

Same safety concerns. Same insights. But this time, she created a moment that stuck.

A home health aide was struggling to get families to follow through on her care recommendations. Her detailed instructions were getting lost in the chaos of family life. So she started doing something different.

Instead of just handing over written care plans, she began each family meeting with a simple story: "Yesterday, Mr. Peterson was able to make his own coffee for the first time in months because we practiced this routine." Then she'd explain the specific steps. Suddenly, families were actually implementing her suggestions.

The medical facts mattered, but the human moment made them unforgettable.

What I want you to understand: being memorable requires intention, not theatrics or drama. Sometimes it's asking the right question. Sometimes it's sharing a story. Sometimes it's knowing when to pause and let silence do the work.

Think of it less like fireworks and more like focus.

A daycare director figured this out when she realized her parent communications were solid but forgettable. She was sending detailed weekly newsletters that nobody read. So she switched to one thing: every Friday, she'd text parents a single photo with one sentence about their child's "spotlight moment" that week.

Parents started asking specifically about those moments. They'd reference them in pick-up conversations. One photo did more than ten newsletters ever had.

I learned this lesson when I was trying to get buy-in for a process improvement project. I kept presenting spreadsheets showing efficiency gains. People would nod politely and nothing would change.

Finally, I tried a different approach. In my next presentation, I opened with: "We're losing the equivalent of one full employee's time every single week to this broken process. That's like paying someone's full salary to accomplish nothing."

You could hear a pin drop. They approved the project that day.

Same data. Different delivery. The difference was creating a moment that made the abstract feel real.

A software developer learned this when she stopped trying to out-talk the louder engineers in her team meetings. Instead, she made it a rule to ask one pointed question that would shift the entire discussion. Over time, people started looking for her input. They'd wait to hear what she was going to ask because they knew it would be worth considering.

She wasn't the loudest voice anymore. She was the most valuable one.

But here's the caution: don't create drama for the sake of drama to be unforgettable. If you make noise without substance, people see through it immediately. The goal is to align your presence with your purpose.

You want to lift your work out of the blur so it actually lands where it needs to.

A doctor's technician told me something that stuck with me: "The doctors don't remember every case update I give them. But they remember the ones that made them stop what they were doing and really listen."

That's the level you're aiming for. Not constant attention-seeking, but strategic moments that break through the noise when it matters most.

In your next important conversation, instead of trying to share everything you know, focus on creating one moment of clarity that people will carry with them. Whether it's a surprising insight, a memorable phrase, or a story that brings your point to life.

Stop being comprehensive and forgettable. Start being focused and unforgettable.

In a world of endless information and shrinking attention spans, the woman who wins isn't the one who talks the most. It's the one who makes herself impossible to forget.

Your competence gets you in the room. Being unforgettable keeps you there.

And when people can't forget you, they can't ignore you either.

38

PICK YOUR BATTLES — AND WIN THEM

There's this thing women do that drives me absolutely crazy, mostly because I spent years doing it myself.

We shrink. We make ourselves smaller, quieter, less threatening, less visible. And we do it automatically, without even realizing we're doing it.

You walk into a meeting and immediately take the chair farthest from the head of the table. You have a brilliant idea but you frame it as a question instead of a statement. You accomplish something significant and you credit everyone else before mentioning your own contribution. You literally take up less physical space, pulling your arms in, making yourself compact, trying not to be too much.

Too much of what? Too much of anything. Too smart, too ambitious, too confident, too visible.

I watched myself do this in a video of a presentation I'd given. I was horrified. I kept apologizing before making points. "This might be wrong, but..." "I'm not sure if this makes sense..." I physically backed away from the front of the room when I wasn't actively speaking. I made my body language as small and non-threatening as possible.

And I wondered why people didn't see me as leadership material.

Because I wasn't showing up like a leader. I was showing up like someone apologizing for being in the room.

The thing is, men almost never do this. Watch men in professional settings. They spread out. They take up space. They state their ideas as facts, not questions. They claim credit for their work directly and unapologetically.

Nobody taught them to make themselves smaller. They learned to take up exactly as much space as they wanted, sometimes more.

Meanwhile, we've been taught our whole lives that taking up space is rude. That confidence is arrogance. That claiming credit is bragging. That we should defer, deflect, diminish ourselves to make others comfortable.

And it's destroying our careers.

This connects to everything we've discussed about visibility and ownership. You can't be visible if you're constantly shrinking. You can't own your accomplishments if you're deflecting credit to everyone else.

Think about how Jacinda Ardern led New Zealand. She never made herself small to make others comfortable. She showed up fully, took up space, and led with confidence.

That's what we're talking about. Not aggressive dominance. Just refusing to shrink.

So here's what making yourself small actually looks like, and you need to stop doing all of it.

Stop starting statements with "This might be stupid, but..." or "I'm not sure if this makes sense..." Your idea either makes sense or it doesn't, but preemptively apologizing for it guarantees nobody takes it seriously.

Stop physically making yourself smaller. Sit at the table, not in chairs against the wall. Uncross your arms. Take up the space your chair offers instead of perching on the edge like you're about to leave.

Stop deflecting credit. When someone praises your work, say "thank you" and own it. Not "Oh, the team did most of it" or "I just got lucky with timing." You did the work. Claim it.

Stop turning statements into questions. "I think we should pursue option A" is stronger than "What if we maybe considered option A?" Say what you mean directly.

Stop over-apologizing. You don't need to say sorry for speaking up, for having an opinion, or for taking up space you have every right to occupy.

I advised a colleague who had this habit of starting every sentence in meetings with "Sorry, but..." She'd interrupt herself with apologies. "Sorry, can I add something?" "Sorry, I have a thought on this."

We worked on eliminating those apologies for just one month. Just removing unnecessary "sorry" from her vocabulary.

Her manager's feedback at the end of that month? "Angela's really come into her own lately. She's showing real leadership presence."

Nothing else had changed. Same person, same competence, same contributions. She just stopped apologizing for having them.

The physical space thing matters too. I started paying attention to how I positioned myself in rooms. Instead of taking the back seat, I'd sit at the table. Instead of making myself compact, I'd sit up straight and use open body language. Instead of backing away when I finished speaking, I'd stay at the front.

The difference in how people responded was immediate. Not because they consciously noticed my body language, but because humans read these signals instinctively. When you take up space confidently, people subconsciously register you as someone with authority.

Think about where you're currently making yourself small. Do you apologize before sharing ideas? Do you physically shrink in meetings? Do you deflect credit for your work?

Pick one habit to change this week. Just one. Maybe it's eliminating apologetic qualifiers. Maybe it's sitting at the table instead of against the wall. Maybe it's claiming credit directly when someone praises your work.

Notice what happens when you stop shrinking. I'm willing to bet people take you more seriously almost immediately.

Because here's what I've learned: the space you don't claim, someone else will. The credit you deflect, someone else will collect. The visibility you shrink from, someone else will grab.

You're not being respectful by making yourself small. You're being invisible.

And invisible people don't get promoted. They don't get opportunities. They don't get to shape decisions or lead initiatives or change anything meaningful.

You have every right to take up space. Every right to own your accomplishments. Every right to speak with confidence about ideas you've thought through.

Stop apologizing for it. Stop qualifying it. Stop shrinking it.

Show up fully. Take your space. Own your work.

Because the woman who makes herself small to make others comfortable is the woman who gets overlooked. The woman who shows up fully, unapologetically, confidently? She's the woman who gets remembered.

39

THEY WANT YOU TO
CRACK—DON'T

You know that feeling when someone says something designed to get under your skin? A sarcastic comment about your timeline being "optimistic." An interruption right when you're making your strongest point. A subtle dig about your "ambition."

Your blood pressure spikes. Your face gets hot. Every instinct screams at you to fire back.

Stop. Right there. That's exactly what they want.

I watched a woman completely destroy her credibility in less than thirty seconds. She was presenting quarterly results to leadership. Solid numbers, clear insights, obviously knew her material. Then one executive made a sarcastic comment about whether her projections were "realistic."

She took the bait. Got defensive, started over-explaining, voice got higher and faster. By the time she finished, everyone in that room had dismissed everything she'd said. Not because her work wasn't good. Because she let them see her crack.

The executive who made the comment? He sat back with a satisfied look. He got exactly what he wanted.

This happens all the time. Someone makes a cutting remark hoping you'll snap. A boss throws last-minute changes at you to see if you'll crack under pressure. A colleague brings up old grievances right before important events.

They're fishing for your reaction. And the moment you give them what they want, you've lost.

Think about the last time someone successfully rattled you. What did they say? How did you respond? Now imagine that same scenario, but this time you stay completely calm. How different would the outcome have been?

The difference would have changed everything.

An emergency room nurse told me that early in her career, she'd get defensive when patients questioned her competence or blamed her for wait times. Then she learned something that transformed her career: the calmest person in chaos becomes the one everyone looks to for leadership.

Now when someone starts yelling, she doesn't match their energy. She lowers her voice. She stays steady. And suddenly, she's the one controlling the entire situation, not the person having the meltdown.

Start noticing every time someone tries to rile you up. The snide comment, the interruption, the passive-aggressive text. When you feel that spike of irritation, you've got three moves.

Pause and breathe. Silence unsettles people way more than shouting does. Name the behavior calmly: "I'm going to finish my thought first." Redirect with purpose: "The real issue we need to address is..."

Pick one technique and watch how differently people respond when you refuse to take their bait.

Sometimes you need to disrupt things yourself, but on your terms, not as a reaction. When a project is moving too fast without proper vetting, a well-timed question like "Have we considered how this impacts existing customers?" creates productive disruption. You're not being obstructive. You're being thorough.

The key is framing your disruption as concern for the outcome, not opposition to people.

A social worker dealing with a family that kept dodging important conversations tried something different. She showed up and said, "I'm wondering if you've decided this process isn't worth your time." That gentle disruption broke through weeks of avoidance.

That's controlled provocation. Agitating on purpose, not being agitated.

The difference between reacting and choosing is everything. When someone tries to rattle you, ask yourself: Am I reacting to their move, or choosing my own response?

If it's reaction, hold steady. If it's choice, lean in with intention.

Look around your workplace. Notice who loses their cool when pressured and who stays steady. Which group has more influence? The double standard exists. A man who gets heated is "passionate." A woman who shows the same emotion gets labeled "difficult" or "emotional." Pretending that doesn't exist won't protect you from it. Mastering your composure will.

Think of every attempt to rattle you as a test. They're watching to see if you'll slip. Your calm becomes your armor.

Some people use chaos as their regular tactic. The manager who creates artificial urgency before every deadline. The colleague who brings up conflicts right before big presentations. Once you see the pattern, you stop falling for it.

Your goal isn't to play their game better. It's to play a different game entirely. Stay steady when they expect you to react. Choose your disruptions when they expect you to stay quiet.

The calmest person in the room is often the most powerful one. Not because they're passive, but because they're in complete control of their own responses.

People will try to throw you off balance. They'll poke and provoke and stir up drama. Don't give them what they want.

Keep your cool. And when you do choose to shake things up, do it with precision and perfect timing.

Stop reacting to their provocations. Start choosing your own responses.

Because the woman who can't be rattled is the woman who can't be controlled.

40

DON'T ACCEPT HELP YOU CAN'T AFFORD TO REPAY

I watched a colleague get trapped in the slowest, quietest way possible.

Her boss offered to "help" her land a big job by making introductions. No strings attached, he said. Just wanted to support her success. She was grateful, said yes, felt lucky to have such a supportive manager.

Three months later, when she wanted to push back on an unreasonable timeline, he reminded her about those introductions. When she tried to take time off, he mentioned how much he'd invested in her career. When she got a job offer from another company, he made it clear she owed him loyalty after everything he'd done.

That "free" help? It cost her the ability to make her own choices.

You've felt this trap closing around you too. Someone covers your shift, puts in a good word, handles a difficult conversation. And suddenly you're walking on eggshells, afraid to disappoint them, unable to say no when they need something.

Nothing is ever truly free. Every gift, every favor, every shortcut comes with a price tag. Sometimes it's light: mutual goodwill you're genuinely happy to return. Sometimes it's heavy: your independence, your voice, your freedom to choose.

Look back at the last six months. Where did someone's "generosity" end up costing you more than you bargained for? Understanding how this works is the difference between building power and accidentally giving it away.

A pharmacy technician thought she'd hit the jackpot when her supervisor offered to cover her weekend shifts "no strings attached." For three months, she felt grateful. Then performance review time came. Suddenly her supervisor was reminding her about all those weekends, suggesting she owed him loyalty on scheduling decisions, implying she should be "more flexible" about overtime.

That wasn't generosity. That was an investment in future control.

Before you accept anything that seems "free," ask yourself: What's the real cost here? What might this person expect in return? Am I willing to pay that price?

But there's a flip side. You can use strategic generosity to build your own influence and reputation.

An administrative assistant started creating training materials for new hires. She didn't get paid extra, and it took hours of her own time. But within a year, the manager was asking her to lead orientation sessions. Her "free" contribution positioned her as a leader and expert.

That's strategic giving. She invested her time in something that built her reputation and visibility.

Think about your workplace. Where could you offer something valuable that would position you as indispensable? What knowledge do you have that others need? What problem could you solve that would get you noticed by the right people?

Pick one thing and make it happen.

Here's your filter for any "opportunity" that comes your way: Ask yourself, "Is this positioning me or weakening me?"

If it builds your visibility, expertise, or future opportunities, lean in. If it creates dependence, obligation, or loss of control, step back.

Every time someone offers you something or asks you to do something "as a favor," pause. Don't answer immediately. Ask yourself those questions. Then decide.

A social worker used to say yes to every committee, every extra project, every request for help. She thought being helpful would advance her career. Instead, she became the go-to person for thankless tasks while others got promoted around her.

Now she has a simple rule: she'll only take on extra work if it either develops a skill she wants to build or connects her with people who can influence her career.

Same willingness to contribute, but now it's strategic instead of scattered.

This also means protecting yourself from guilt-based manipulation. The "I thought you were a team player" comments when you set boundaries. The "After everything I've done for you" reminders when you don't comply with unreasonable requests.

That's not gratitude they're asking for. That's control.

You don't owe anyone your independence in exchange for their help.

Think about all the ways you've been giving your time and energy lately. Now think about what you've gotten back: reputation, skills, connections, opportunities. If those feel wildly unbalanced, you're giving yourself away instead of investing yourself strategically.

Generosity is powerful, but only when it's intentional. Give in ways that build your brand. Refuse gifts that come with invisible strings.

Protect yourself by seeing the real price of "free." Position yourself by making your generosity count.

Because the moment you understand that everything has a cost, you can start making sure you're the one setting the terms.

Stop accepting help that comes with hidden price tags. Start giving strategically in ways that build your power.

And when you control the terms, you control the outcome.

41

BUILD YOUR BRAND,
NOT THEIRS

You're never going to win at being someone else.

I don't care how hard you try, how much you study their moves, or how perfectly you replicate their approach. You will lose that game every single time because you're competing against a memory, and memories get better with time while you're stuck being compared to a fantasy.

A brilliant woman took over a department after a beloved manager retired. Everyone adored him. He remembered birthdays, knew everyone's kids' names, had this warm, hands-on style that made people feel seen.

She spent six months trying to be him. Forcing warmth that didn't come naturally. Remembering details that exhausted her. Attempting to replicate his management approach down to the weekly donuts he brought in.

And people said, "She's nice, but she's not really him."

She was invisible. Not because she wasn't capable. She was arguably more capable. But because she was playing his game instead of building her own.

Every minute you spend trying to fill someone else's shoes is a minute you're not building your own path. And the comparison will never end as long as you're playing their game.

Think about how you introduce yourself at work. Do you say "I'm in Rachel's old role" or "I took over from Michael"? That's the trap. You're defining yourself by someone else's legacy instead of creating your own.

The moment you stop trying to be like your predecessor and start showing who you actually are, everything shifts. People stop the constant comparison because you've created something entirely new to evaluate.

That department manager finally had enough. She brought her own strengths to the role: better systems, clearer communication protocols, stronger boundaries with difficult stakeholders. Different approach. Different style. Incredibly effective.

Within three months, people stopped saying "Well, Tom used to do it this way" because she'd built something that had her stamp on it. Her brand. Her approach. Her results.

I know you've felt this pressure too. This constant feeling that you need to be like someone else to be taken seriously. Maybe it's at work, maybe in your family, maybe in how you approach leadership.

The world doesn't need another version of someone who already existed. It needs the first version of who you're becoming.

Identify one area where you've been following someone else's script. Maybe it's how you run meetings, how you handle conflict, or how you communicate with your team. What would your version look like?

A restaurant manager tried for months to match her predecessor's "tough love" style. Everyone talked about how he could motivate through intensity and high standards. She forced herself to be harder, more demanding, more intense than felt natural.

It was exhausting and it didn't work.

Then she tried something radical: she managed the way she naturally managed. More collaborative. More focused on training than yelling. More emphasis on building skills than demanding perfection.

Different? Absolutely. Effective? Even more so than her predecessor.

This isn't just about work. Are you trying to be the kind of mother your mom was? The kind of friend someone else is? The kind of partner that worked for someone else's relationship?

Stop copying their playbook and start writing your own.

Because when you're authentic, your energy changes. People feel that shift. They respond to the confidence of someone who knows who they are instead of someone who's pretending to be someone else.

There's also a practical danger that nobody talks about. When you tie your identity to someone else's legacy, what happens when their reputation changes? When they move on? When people get tired of the comparison?

If you haven't built your own foundation, you fall with theirs.

I know someone who spent years being known as "David's protégé" at her firm. She was brilliant, but everyone saw her as an extension of his brand. When he left for another company, she suddenly became invisible. She had to rebuild from scratch because she'd never established herself as her own entity.

Don't make that mistake.

Building your own brand doesn't mean rejecting everything that came before. You can honor what worked while creating something uniquely yours. But the emphasis needs to be on your strengths, your approach, your authentic leadership style.

The next time someone compares you to your predecessor or asks you to do something "the way it used to be done," don't automatically comply. Instead, say something like: "I can see why that worked well. Here's how I'd approach it." Then do it your way.

Start small. Maybe it's changing how you structure a weekly meeting. Maybe it's introducing a new communication format. Maybe it's bringing your natural problem-solving style to a challenge instead of asking "what would they have done?"

Watch what happens when you stop apologizing for not being them and start celebrating being you.

You don't rise by filling someone else's shoes. You rise by building your own path. Creating your own brand. Showing people what you bring to the table that nobody else can replicate.

Because when you're trying to be someone else, you're robbing the world of who you actually are. And that person? She's the one with the real power.

Stop trying to be a better version of them. Start being the best version of you.

42

DISMANTLE THE NETWORK BEFORE THE NETWORKS AGAINST YOU

Someone is building a coalition against you right now, and you're probably missing it.

They're not doing it loudly. They're not announcing it in meetings or sending threatening emails. They're doing it quietly in coffee conversations and sidebar chats after meetings, as carefully worded complaints to the right ears. They're building support, gathering allies, positioning themselves as the reasonable alternative to you.

And if you wait until they're organized? You've already lost.

When someone is organizing against you, their power comes from their network. And you can dismantle that network before they use it to undermine you.

This is defensive strategy, not offensive warfare. This is about protecting your position before someone uses their organized support to take it from you.

Women face this differently than men do. When a man builds a coalition, he's "developing leadership" or "building consensus." When we do it, we're "being political" or "forming cliques." And when someone builds a coalition against us? We're told we're "not collaborative enough" or "not a team player."

The rules are different. But the tactics still work.

People don't usually come for you alone. They build support first. They need validation, backup, the appearance of representing "the group" rather than just their own agenda. That network is their power source.

Your move? Identify it early. Disrupt it strategically. Scatter it before it's weaponized against you.

Think about your workplace right now. Is there someone who's been unusually vocal about "concerns" lately? Someone who's suddenly very interested in gathering opinions about decisions you've made? Someone positioning themselves as the voice of "what everyone's really thinking"?

That's not casual conversation. That's network building.

I watched this play out in a department where a project manager felt threatened by a new director. She couldn't challenge the director directly, wrong optics, wrong power differential. So she spent three months quietly building a coalition. Lunches with key team members. Sympathetic listening sessions about "how things used to be better." Careful questions in meetings that made the director's decisions seem questionable.

By the time the director realized what was happening, half the team had already been positioned as "her people" versus "the director's agenda."

The director lost that battle because she didn't see the network forming until it was already working against her.

Don't make that mistake.

Watch for pattern changes. Someone who never used to have coffee
with certain colleagues is suddenly meeting them regularly. Someone's
having a lot of "quick sidebar" conversations after group meetings.

Listen for language shifts. When someone starts using phrases like
"we've been talking" or "people are saying" or "there's concern among
the team," they're signaling that they've built consensus, real or man-
ufactured, against something. Usually against you.

Notice alliance formations. Who's suddenly sitting together in meetings? Who's backing each other's points? Those aren't random social
patterns. Those are coordinated behaviors.

Now here's the defensive strategy: you don't attack the person building the network. That makes you look paranoid or threatened.
Instead, you disrupt the network itself.

How? You rebuild direct relationships with the people they're
recruiting.

A nurse manager figured this out when she noticed a senior nurse
gathering support against a new protocol. Instead of confronting the
senior nurse, she scheduled individual conversations with each team
member. Not to complain about the senior nurse, but to genuinely
hear concerns, explain the reasoning behind changes, and build individual relationships.

Within two weeks, the coalition dissolved. Not because the senior
nurse stopped trying, but because the network she was building had
stronger connections elsewhere.

Map who talks to whom in your environment. Not the org chart, the actual influence patterns. Who has coffee with whom? Who checks in with whom? You'll see the networks clearly once you pay attention.

Then ask yourself: are any of these networks forming around opposition to something you're doing? Are they being built strategically by someone who sees you as a threat?

If yes, don't panic. But don't ignore it either.

Strengthen your own direct relationships with the people in that forming network. Not to badmouth anyone, not to create drama, but to make sure you're not allowing someone else to control the narrative about you.

A retail manager learned this when an assistant manager started gathering the team against her. Instead of addressing it head-on, she started doing what she should have been doing all along: actually talking to her team members individually, understanding their concerns, showing up for them in ways that mattered.

The assistant manager's network fell apart because the people in it had their own direct positive experiences that contradicted the narrative being built.

Sometimes people organize against you not because you're wrong, but because you're threatening their position, their comfort, or their control. That's not your failure. That's workplace reality.

But if you let them organize unopposed, their perception becomes the group's reality.

Dismantle the network by making their story irrelevant. Build stronger connections. Create your own narrative through direct relationships and consistent action. Make it impossible for someone to speak for "the group" because the group has their own direct experience with you.

Networks built on complaints and grievances are fragile. They only hold together as long as the architect keeps feeding them. Networks built on genuine connection and mutual respect? Those are the ones that last.

So yes, watch for people building support against you. Recognize the pattern early. But don't fight it with confrontation.

Fight it by being so directly connected to people that no intermediary can come between you and reality.

Stop letting others control the narrative about you. Start building relationships that make their stories irrelevant.

43

WIN LOYALTY, NOT JUST COMPLIANCE

People don't quit bad jobs. They quit bad managers.

And if you're in any kind of leadership role, whether managing a team, running a department, leading a shift, or supervising a crew, you need to hear this: your people are doing what you tell them to do, but that doesn't mean they're actually with you.

There's a massive difference between compliance and loyalty. Compliance is what happens when people follow your instructions because they have to. Loyalty is what happens when they follow you because they want to see you succeed.

One evaporates the second you turn your back. The other protects you even when you're not in the room.

Women leaders get judged on this differently than men do. A male manager can be demanding and cold and he's "results-oriented" or "no-nonsense." A woman who manages the same way? She's "a bitch" or "difficult to work for."

Meanwhile, when we try to build genuine connections with our teams, we risk being labeled "too soft" or "not tough enough for leadership." We're expected to be both warm and commanding, both nurturing and authoritative, a balance men never have to strike.

Think about the best manager you ever had. It probably wasn't the one who demanded the most or had the strictest rules. It was probably the one who made you feel seen, heard, and valued. The one who remembered what mattered to you. The one who had your back when things got difficult.

That wasn't an accident. That was strategy.

Here's a quick example: two shift supervisors at a hospital. The first one ran her floor by the book. Strict schedules, rigid protocols, no exceptions. Everything happened exactly on time when she was on duty, but the nursing staff would literally hide when they saw her coming.

The second supervisor had the same standards and expectations. But she knew that one nurse was studying for her RN exam. She knew that another's father was ill. She knew that someone's daughter just made the varsity basketball team. She checked in on people. She celebrated their wins. She had their backs when difficult patients or families got abusive.

Guess which supervisor people actually wanted to pick up extra shifts for? Guess whose team had lower turnover and better patient outcomes?

If you're in a leadership position and people only perform when you're watching, you don't have influence. You have surveillance. And the moment you're not looking, everything falls apart.

Think about your own team. When people think about working with you, what do they actually feel? Energized or exhausted? Respected or dismissed? Do they want to see you succeed, or are they just counting down until they can transfer?

Be brutally honest with yourself here. That emotional residue you leave behind becomes your reputation. And your reputation becomes your real power.

This doesn't mean you have to be everyone's best friend or lower your standards to be liked. It means you understand that people are moved by how you make them feel, not just by what you demand from them.

A restaurant manager was struggling with constant staff turnover. She couldn't figure out why people kept quitting even though the pay was competitive. Then she watched security footage one day and realized something uncomfortable. She was efficient, professional, and fair. But she was also completely cold. No warmth, no personal connection, no acknowledgment of her staff as actual human beings.

She started small. Learning names of people's kids. Asking how someone's class went. Noticing when someone seemed off and checking in. Not in a fake, forced way, but genuinely.

Within three months, turnover dropped by sixty percent. Same restaurant, same job, same manager. Different emotional environment.

Identify the five people whose support matters most to your success. Think about the last time you genuinely invested in those relationships. Not asked for something, not gave an instruction, but actually showed interest in their success and wellbeing.

If you're seeing gaps, start there.

A veterinary practice owner transformed her entire clinic culture by making one simple change. Instead of just running through the schedule and task lists during morning huddles, she started spending two minutes asking about people's lives.

"How's your mom doing after her surgery?" "Did your son's science fair project go well?" "Are you still training for that half marathon?"

Those tiny conversations built real connections. Her staff started communicating more openly, covering for each other proactively, and treating customers better because they felt genuinely cared for themselves.

That's what sustainable influence looks like. People choose to support you because they want to, not because they have to.

But don't confuse genuine connection with manipulation. You've probably worked with someone who was all charm and flattery but never actually followed through on promises or treated people fairly behind closed doors.

That's not loyalty building. That's manipulation. And people see through it eventually.

Real loyalty comes from consistency. Being fair, reliable, and respectful even when it's inconvenient. Especially when it's inconvenient.

A construction site supervisor inherited a crew that had been through three supervisors in two years. They were defensive, uncooperative, and frankly didn't trust anyone in a leadership position.

She didn't try to win them over with big speeches or false promises. She just showed up every day, treated people with respect, listened to their safety concerns, and made sure credit went to the people who actually did the work. It took months, but eventually the crew started trusting her. Not because she was charismatic, but because she was consistent.

Think about who in your circle feels connected enough to defend you when you're not in the room. Who repeats your ideas and gives you credit? Who protects your reputation when others question it?

If the answer is "not many people," you've got work to do. And that's okay. Now you know where to focus.

Your title might give you temporary authority, but genuine connection gives you lasting power. When you've built real loyalty, people work harder for you, communicate more openly with you, and protect your interests even when you're not around.

Compliance can be forced. Loyalty has to be earned.

And loyalty is what makes your influence outlast any job title, any role change, any organizational restructuring you'll ever experience.

Start treating your people like human beings with lives, concerns, and dreams outside of work. Learn what matters to them. Show up for them consistently. Give credit generously. Have their backs when things get difficult.

Not because you're trying to manipulate them into working harder. Because you understand that people who feel genuinely valued become your strongest allies.

Stop managing through fear and surveillance. Start leading through connection and consistency.

And when people genuinely want to see you win, you've got something that can never be taken away from you, no matter how the org chart changes or what title you hold.

44

MIRROR THEM TO MASTER THEM

The reason you instantly click with some people and clash with others isn't chemistry. It's mirroring.

And once you understand how mirroring works, you can use it to build instant connection with anyone or expose bad behavior without ever having to be the one who calls it out directly.

When you meet someone and feel like you "just get each other," what's actually happening is one of you is unconsciously matching the other's energy, pace, communication style, or body language. Your brain reads that similarity as safety and connection.

Smart leaders use this deliberately. Not to manipulate, but to create genuine rapport and to protect themselves from people who are trying to throw them off balance.

Women have been doing this our whole lives. We've been trained to mirror and adapt since childhood. "Read the room." "Don't be too much." "Match their energy." We've been unconsciously mirroring men's communication styles, adjusting our voices, modulating our presence to make others comfortable.

The difference is, we're going to start doing it consciously. Strategically. For our benefit, not just theirs.

You're meeting with a potential buyer who speaks slowly and thoughtfully, taking long pauses between sentences. Most people would jump in to fill those silences with rapid explanations. But if you match their pace instead? Slow down your delivery, leave space for their processing time, mirror their thoughtful energy?

Suddenly they lean in. They feel understood. They trust you because your communication style matches theirs.

That's strategic mirroring. Reading the room and adjusting your energy to create connection.

Now here's where it gets really useful. Say you're working with someone who constantly interrupts. Not just you, but everyone. Instead of calling them out directly or complaining to management, you try something different.

The next time they cut you off mid-sentence, you calmly do the same thing back to them. Just once. Just enough for the room to notice.

Watch what happens. Suddenly everyone sees the interrupting behavior clearly because it's being reflected back. Sometimes showing people their own behavior is more powerful than any conversation you could have about respect or professionalism.

A dental hygienist used this technique with a dentist who had a habit of making dismissive comments about her clinical observations. Instead of arguing or getting defensive, she started responding to his suggestions with the same dismissive tone he used with her.

"Hmm, interesting theory," delivered with his exact inflection.

It only took twice before he stopped completely. He heard how he sounded when it was reflected back to him, and he didn't like it.

Think about your last difficult interaction at work. Did you immediately jump to defending yourself or explaining why the other person was wrong? What would have happened if you'd simply reflected their energy back to them instead? Not escalating it, just showing them what they were bringing to the conversation?

Mirror someone's communication style to build rapport. If they're detail-oriented, get specific with your responses. If they're big-picture focused, stay high-level. Notice how much easier the conversation becomes when you're speaking their language.

Mirror someone's body language during an important conversation. If they lean back, you lean back. If they use hand gestures while talking, you incorporate some too. It creates subconscious connection that makes people more receptive to what you're saying.

And here's the advanced move: if someone's being unreasonable or disruptive, mirror their behavior just enough to make it visible to others. But do this sparingly and with complete control. You're not trying to escalate the situation. You're trying to illuminate what's happening.

A preschool teacher figured out she could calm an entire classroom of overstimulated kids just by consistently modeling the energy she wanted to see. Instead of trying to talk over their excitement, she would speak more quietly. Instead of rushing around, she would move slowly and deliberately.

The kids naturally started matching her calm because that's how powerful mirroring can be. We're wired to sync up with the energy around us.

But don't mirror unconsciously. If someone's bringing chaotic energy and you just absorb it and reflect it back without thinking, you'll make everything worse.

Mastery means choosing what to reflect.

You deliberately mirror positive energy and productive behaviors to build connection. You strategically mirror negative behaviors only when it serves a specific purpose, like exposing bad behavior or setting a boundary.

Some people will try to throw you off balance by suddenly shifting their energy. They'll go from calm to aggressive, or warm to cold, hoping you'll mirror their chaos and lose your composure.

When you recognize this happening, hold your own center. Don't let their energy shifts control yours. That's the difference between reactive mirroring and strategic mirroring.

A restaurant manager learned this lesson when dealing with an employee who would flip between being cooperative and combative depending on his mood. For months, she found herself matching his energy shifts, getting frustrated when he got frustrated, being cold when he was cold.

Once she recognized the pattern, she stopped mirroring his chaos. She stayed consistent regardless of what energy he brought. It took about two weeks, but he eventually started matching her steady energy instead of her matching his volatility.

Pay attention to your automatic mirroring patterns. When someone gets stressed, do you automatically mirror their stress? When someone speaks in a confrontational tone, do you match it without thinking?

Notice these unconscious responses so you can start making conscious choices instead.

A physical therapist transformed her patient relationships by paying attention to how each person communicated and mirroring it back. Some patients wanted detailed explanations of every exercise. Others just wanted the basics and trusted her expertise. Some needed encouragement and positivity. Others responded better to straight-forward, no-nonsense coaching.

She stopped using the same approach with everyone and started matching each person's communication style. Her patient satisfaction scores went up significantly because people felt truly understood.

That's the power of conscious mirroring. Connection grows when you mirror what's working. Boundaries hold when you mirror what's not. And you stay in control because you're choosing what gets reflected.

You don't have to fight every battle head-on. Sometimes the smartest move is to hold up a mirror and let people see themselves clearly.

Stop unconsciously adapting to everyone else's energy. Start consciously choosing what you reflect.

Match their communication style to build trust. Mirror their body language to create rapport. Reflect their negative behavior back just enough to expose it without becoming the villain who called them out.

And when you master the mirror, you can build connection with anyone and set boundaries without ever having to be the bad guy in the story.

45

PACE YOUR VISION OR LOSE YOUR INFLUENCE

Your brilliant plan to fix everything at once is probably why people are resisting you, not supporting you.

You can see exactly what needs to change. The inefficiencies are obvious. The outdated systems are frustrating. The better way forward is crystal clear in your mind.

So you announce your comprehensive plan to overhaul everything, expecting people to be excited about finally fixing what's been broken for so long.

Instead? Panic. Pushback. Quiet conversations about how you're "trying to change everything" or "moving too fast."

People say they want change, but their brains are wired for stability. Too much transformation at once feels like a threat, not an opportunity. And when people feel threatened, they resist. Even when your ideas are good.

Your influence doesn't come from having the best vision. It comes from pacing that vision so people can actually follow you.

Think about the last time you stepped into a leadership role and saw ten things that needed immediate fixing. What happened when you tried to tackle them all at once?

People dug in their heels. They questioned your judgment. They found reasons why "it won't work here" or "we've always done it this way." Not because your ideas were bad, but because you overwhelmed them with too much change too fast.

Now picture a different approach. You pick one visible problem and fix it really well. People see the positive results. They start to trust your judgment. Then you tackle the next issue. And then the next.

By the time you're ready to implement the bigger changes, your team is asking when you can start because you've proven you know what you're doing.

A physical therapy clinic owner learned this lesson the hard way. She took over a practice running on systems from the 1990s. Paper charts, phone call appointment reminders, handwritten intake forms.

She wanted to modernize everything immediately. New software, digital records, online scheduling, automated communications. She announced the full transformation plan at a staff meeting.

Her team nearly revolted. Too much. Too fast. Too overwhelming.

So she backed up and started over. First change? Digital appointment confirmations instead of phone calls. Just that one thing. It saved the front desk staff thirty minutes every single day. They were thrilled.

Next change? Streamlined the intake paperwork patients filled out. Another clear win. Better for patients, easier for staff.

By the time she proposed the major software upgrade six months later, her team was asking when they could start training because they'd learned to trust her judgment.

Consider a change you want to make right now. Instead of overwhelming everyone with your full vision, what's the smallest first step that would prove progress is possible? Figure out what the second step would be. And the third.

You're not dumbing down your vision or compromising your standards. You're building the runway so others can take off with you.

A property manager used this approach when she wanted to improve how the team handled difficult owners. Instead of implementing a whole new protocol at once, she started by changing just one thing: how they responded when an owner called upset about a bill or an issue.

She taught her front desk staff one new phrase and one new process for those specific calls. It worked beautifully. Fewer escalations, happier owners, less stressed staff.

Then she moved to the next improvement repeating the process of introducing change. Each change was small enough to master before adding the next layer.

Within a year, the entire service experience had transformed. But nobody felt overwhelmed because each step was manageable and clearly beneficial.

Other people use this same technique to push agendas you might not support. That colleague who keeps suggesting "just one small change" every few weeks? They might be quietly reshaping your entire work environment without you noticing.

Pay attention to patterns. Big changes rarely happen all at once in obvious ways. They happen drip by drip, small shift by small shift, until suddenly everything looks different.

Pick the one piece that will create the most visible positive impact. Get that working smoothly. Let people experience the benefit. Then move to the next piece.

A restaurant manager learned this when she wanted to improve how her team handled the dinner rush. Instead of overhauling the entire system, she started with one bottleneck: how they processed drink orders during peak times.

She changed just that one workflow. Faster service, fewer mistakes, happier customers. Her team saw it work. So when she suggested the next improvement to food runner coordination, they were on board immediately.

That's change that sticks because it feels organic, not forced.

Think about the last time you tried to implement multiple changes at once. How did people respond? What would have happened if you'd tackled them one at a time instead? The resistance would have been cut in half.

Identify one change you want to make. Break it down into the smallest possible steps. Implement only the first step. Let people adjust and see the benefit before you move to step two.

Don't burn out your own influence by pushing too hard too fast. You might be right about everything that needs to change. Being right doesn't matter if people won't follow you.

Respect the human need for stability. When you give people space to adjust, they're less likely to resist or sabotage your efforts. When you prove each step works before moving to the next, you build credibility instead of burning it.

Change is power, but only if you can bring people along with you. Push too fast and they'll fight you every step of the way. Pace it strategically and they'll help you build something better.

A construction site supervisor transformed safety compliance on her crew using this exact approach. Instead of implementing all the new safety protocols at once, she started with one highly visible change: mandatory safety glasses for everyone, all the time.

She enforced it consistently. Explained why it mattered. Made it non-negotiable. Once that became habit, she moved to the next protocol. Then the next.

Her crew went from worst safety record to best in the company. Not because she had better ideas than previous supervisors. Because she paced the implementation so her crew could actually follow.

Stop trying to change everything at once. Start building change that actually lasts.

Lead change in steps and you'll keep your influence intact while your vision takes root. Try to change everything simultaneously and watch your credibility crumble along with your relationships.

The leader who changes everything slowly is the one who actually changes everything permanently.

46

YOUR PERFECTION IS MAKING THEM HATE YOU

That flawless image you've been working so hard to maintain? It's actually working against you.

You've been told your whole life that women have to work twice as hard to be seen as half as good. That there's no room for error. That perfect execution is the price of admission to respect and advancement.

And that's exactly the trap. Because perfection doesn't inspire people. It intimidates them. And intimidated people don't become allies. They become critics waiting for you to slip.

Think about that woman at work who seems to have everything together. Perfect presentations, flawless execution, never a hair out of place or a word out of turn. She's impressive, right?

But you don't actually like her very much. And you're not entirely sure why.

I'll tell you why. When someone appears flawless, others project their insecurities onto them. They assume doors open effortlessly, that struggle is foreign, that success just falls into their lap. Whether that's true or not doesn't matter. The perception isolates you and breeds resentment.

Perfection is brittle. It gives people nothing to connect with.

Think about the managers you've actually respected and wanted to follow. They weren't the ones who never made mistakes. They were the ones who owned their mistakes, learned from them, and brought you along for the journey.

Think about three women you genuinely admire. Not just professionally respect, but actually like and want to see succeed. What makes them appealing? It's not their perfection. It's their humanity combined with their competence.

A nurse told me about two doctors she worked with at her hospital. Dr. Perfect never admitted uncertainty, never asked for input, never showed any sign that medicine was challenging. Every decision appeared effortless and absolute.

Dr. Real would sometimes say things like, "This case is tricky. Let me consult with cardiology" or "I learned something new about this treatment last week that might help."

Guess which doctor the entire nursing staff trusted more? Guess which one they'd go to bat for when things got difficult?

Your strength doesn't come from never struggling. It comes from how you handle the struggle when it shows up.

Pick one area where you've been trying to appear effortless. Maybe it's how you run team meetings, how you handle difficult projects, or how you solve problems.

Instead of hiding the effort, acknowledge it strategically.

"This project was more complex than we initially thought, but here's how we adapted." "I had to learn a new system to make this work, and here's what I discovered." "The first version of this approach didn't land right, so we tried something different."

You're not making excuses. You're showing the reality behind results. And that reality makes your success more impressive, not less.

But there's a crucial balance. You're showing effort and process, not weakness or incompetence. There's a huge difference between saying "I struggled with this and couldn't figure it out" versus "I figured out a creative solution when the original plan didn't work."

Frame your humanity in terms of growth, learning, and problem solving. That makes you relatable without undermining your credibility.

Watch out for people who weaponize perfection as a competitive strategy. They present this image of effortless competence specifically designed to make everyone else feel inadequate.

Don't fall for it. That polish usually hides chaos underneath.

A restaurant manager spent months comparing herself to another manager who always seemed calm, organized, perfectly in control. The schedule always worked perfectly. Staff issues resolved smoothly. Everything looked easy.

Later she found out the "perfect" manager was working sixteen hour days, had no personal life, was on anxiety medication, and quietly burning out. The polished exterior was a performance, not reality.

The lesson? Don't chase someone else's performance of perfection. It's usually hiding more struggle than you realize.

Think about one area where you feel pressure to be perfect. What's the reality? The effort. The learning curve. The process. The adjustments you made when things didn't work the first time.

What part of that reality could you share without undermining your credibility? What would make you more relatable instead of less competent?

Start small. Share one piece of your process in a safe conversation and notice how people respond. They'll lean in rather than pull away.

The most powerful leaders don't try to be flawless. They try to be credible. They combine clear competence with visible humanity in a way that makes people want to follow them.

When you appear perfect, you're setting yourself up as a target. People who feel inadequate around you will look for cracks in your armor. They'll wait for you to mess up. They'll hope you fail because your failure would make them feel better about their own imperfections.

But when you show your humanity strategically? When you share your process, your learning, your growth? People root for you instead of against you.

Perfection sparks envy. Authenticity builds loyalty.

Stop trying to be flawless. Start being real, competent, and relatable all at once. That's where your real power lives.

47

QUIT WHILE YOU'RE WINNING

Your biggest enemy right now isn't failure. It's your inability to let success be enough.

You finally land that big customer. You nail the presentation that gets you noticed. You achieve the goal you've been working toward for months. And then, instead of pausing to let that victory settle, you immediately start piling on more.

More follow-ups. More additions. More proof. More evidence that you deserve what you've earned.

When you can't stop proving yourself, your success starts working against you. The client who was thrilled with your work gets overwhelmed by your constant check-ins. The boss who was impressed by your project gets annoyed by your endless additions to it. The victory that should have opened doors starts closing them instead.

You're not building on your success. You're burying it.

I know why you do this. You've been taught that women have to work twice as hard to get half the recognition. That you can't let up for a second or someone will decide you don't deserve what you've earned. That if you're not constantly proving yourself, you'll be forgotten or replaced.

But when you can't stop, people start questioning whether you believe in your own work. Because if you really thought it was good enough, you wouldn't keep adding to it, would you?

The next time you secure a win, resist every instinct to keep adding to it. Document the success clearly. Celebrate it appropriately. Then step back and let it breathe.

There's a huge difference between building momentum and overplaying your hand.

Watch for this pattern in others too. You'll start noticing colleagues who push past their victories and accidentally create resentment. The team member who keeps adding slides to a successful presentation until it becomes bloated and boring. The manager who won respect but then tries to control every tiny detail until people start avoiding her input.

Sometimes you don't need to compete with people who do this. You just need to let them exhaust themselves while you practice strategic restraint.

Think about where in your life you're adding effort not because it's needed, but because you're afraid your win won't hold without constant reinforcement.

Maybe it's following up on emails that already got positive responses. Maybe it's adding unnecessary details to reports that were already approved. Maybe it's continuing to prove a point long after everyone already agrees with you.

When you complete something successfully, sit with that completion. Don't immediately jump to the next addition or improvement.

Let the work speak for itself for at least 24 hours before you decide if anything else is actually needed.

A restaurant server realized she was over-explaining menu items to the point where customers felt overwhelmed rather than helped. She thought detailed descriptions showed expertise. Really, it made people feel like they couldn't make their own decisions.

When she learned to give just enough information and then step back, her tips went up significantly. Customers appreciated her knowledge but also her respect for their autonomy.

Strength isn't only in the pursuit. It's also in the wisdom to know when you've arrived.

Your wins are valid exactly as they are. You don't need to keep stacking evidence on top of evidence. You don't need to chase every opportunity immediately just to prove you can handle it.

Know when enough is enough. Your future self will thank you for the space you create by stopping at the right moment.

48

REFUSE TO BE JUST ONE THING

Here we are. The final power principle.

You've learned to build your own brand instead of copying some-one else's. You've discovered how to dismantle threat networks before they work against you. You've mastered winning loyalty and mirror-ing strategically. You've learned to pace your vision, show strategic humanity, and quit while you're winning.

Now we tackle something that we've all felt at some point. That we are typecast into a particular role by those that want to confine us to what makes them comfortable.

The world is obsessed with putting you in a box. Your power lies in refusing to stay there.

Now I'm going to tell you the most important thing that ties all of this together. The skill that makes every other principle work. The foundation that supports everything you've learned about power.

The moment you let people lock you into one identity, one role, one predictable pattern, your power shrinks to the size of their expectations.

Your colleagues want to label you. "She's the nice one." "She's the detail person." "She's too emotional." "She's too aggressive." Your industry wants to typecast you. Your family wants you to stay exactly who you've always been. Even your friends sometimes get uncomfortable when you show them a side of yourself they haven't seen before.

And if you let them box you in? If you perform just one version of yourself because it's easier than dealing with their confusion when you shift? You're handing them control over who you get to be.

Think about where in your life you feel trapped by other people's expectations. Where are you playing just one role because it's what everyone expects, even though you're capable of so much more?

That's exactly where you need more fluidity.

Predictability makes you vulnerable. When people know exactly how you'll react, they can push your buttons. They can manipulate you. They can use your consistency against you.

But when you're fluid? When you refuse to be just one thing? When they can't quite pin down your next move? This is why boxers constantly bob, weave and move in a fight. Punches don't land. You stay in control.

A physical therapist works with athletes, elderly patients recovering from surgery, and kids with developmental delays. Each population needs something completely different from her.

With athletes, she's direct, competitive, pushing them hard. With elderly patients, she's patient, encouraging, celebrating small wins. With kids, she's playful, creative, making therapy feel like games.

Same woman. Different facets. She doesn't let anyone lock her into "the tough therapist" or "the gentle therapist" because she's both, depending on what the situation needs.

You're not being fake. You're being multifaceted. You have layers. The version of you that shows up for your family isn't less authentic than the version that leads at work. They're both you.

Think about the roles you play: leader, partner, parent, friend, daughter, professional, whatever your list looks like.

Are you trying to blend all these into one consistent personality to make other people comfortable? Or are you giving yourself permission to shift between them as needed?

Notice when you feel the pressure to perform consistency. When someone says "that's not like you" or "you've changed" or "I liked you better when you were more [whatever]."

Those moments? Those are attempts to box you in. And you get to decide whether you stay in that box or break out of it.

Watch out for people who demand consistency from you as a control tactic. "But you never used to speak up like this." "That's not who you are." "You're being difficult."

Translation: "I liked it better when I could predict and control you."

You don't owe anyone a consistent, limited version of yourself just because it makes them comfortable. You're allowed to grow, shift, adapt, and show different parts of yourself in different contexts.

When you stay fluid, when you refuse to be boxed in, some people will be uncomfortable. They'll try to label you inconsistent, unpredictable, complicated.

Let them be uncomfortable. Their discomfort is not your problem to solve.

Think about the women you most admire. They're not one-dimensional. They're complex, surprising, capable of being multiple things at once. Tough and vulnerable. Strategic and spontaneous. Confident and curious.

That complexity is power. That refusal to be simple enough for everyone else to understand easily is strength.

A construction site supervisor stopped apologizing for being "too much" in different contexts. Too direct for people who wanted her softer. Too collaborative for people who wanted her more authoritative. Too strategic for people who wanted her more tactical.

She realized she wasn't too much. She was exactly enough, in all her complexity, and other people's inability to categorize her easily was their limitation, not hers.

So here's my final message to you after these 48 power principles.

Stay fluid. Stay free. Refuse to shrink yourself into one predictable, manageable, easily labeled version of who you are.

You're allowed to be sharp and kind. Strategic and authentic. Ambitious and balanced. Confident and still learning. All of it. At the same time. In different moments. As the situation requires.

The world will keep trying to put you in a box. "She's this type of woman." "She's that kind of leader." "She's too [whatever] for [whatever]."

Let them try. And then show them something they didn't expect.

Your power isn't in being consistent. It's in being authentic, adaptable, and absolutely refusing to be limited by anyone else's narrow vision of who you should be.

You've come this far. You've learned these principles. You've seen how power actually works, not how people pretend it works.

Now go use it. Stay fluid. Stay free. And never, ever let anyone convince you that you have to be just one thing.

The woman who refuses to be boxed in? She's the one who changes the game entirely.

Everything we've covered so far has been about you—your moves, your strategy, your power. And that matters enormously. But the truth is, no woman succeeds in corporate America entirely on her own.

The most powerful women I know didn't just build their skills; they built their circles. They surrounded themselves with people who believed in them, advocated for them, and lifted them higher.

Now it's time to talk about building yours.

Part II

The Network Effect

—————•————— ♀ —————•—————

BUILD YOUR POWER CIRCLE

Why Networking Isn't Enough Anymore

You've heard it a hundred times: "It's not what you know, it's who you know." But here's the truth no one tells you: random connections won't get you promoted. A bloated LinkedIn contact list means nothing if those relationships aren't activated. In today's competitive workplace, especially in male-dominated environments, power, visibility, and access aren't handed out based on performance alone. They're brokered through a strategic web of relationships you intentionally build and maintain.

The Moment I Learned the Real Game

Let me tell you how I learned this firsthand, because it didn't come from a women's leadership seminar or a corporate mentor. It came from a male colleague.

Every few weeks, like clockwork, he'd swing by my office with the same casual question: "Coffee break?" It wasn't unusual, just consistent. Predictable. Over time, I realized something powerful: he always knew what was going on in my world. Not in a nosy way. He was just tuned in. He asked about my projects, congratulated me on promotions before they hit the org chart, and even remembered things about my son, checking in months later like it was second nature.

One day, when we were trying to schedule a catch-up, he laughed and said, "Sorry. I've got three other coffee check-ins on my calendar this week. I make sure I touch base with everyone regularly. It doesn't matter if there's anything big going on. Just a hello or a check in to keep the connection alive."

Then he shared something that stuck with me: "One of my old teammates from years ago is now in the C-suite of a Fortune 100. We've never let more than three months go by without talking. A phone call, a conference check-in, a beer. I don't need anything from him, but I know if I did? All it takes is one call."

That was the moment it clicked. It wasn't about networking. It was about nurturing relationships with intention.

This is where Power Circles come in.

What Is a Power Circle?

A Power Circle is your intentionally cultivated inner circle of influence, comprised of mentors, allies, peers, and rising professionals who play a defined role in expanding your visibility, credibility, opportunities, and career progression. These are not just people you "like" or run into. They are individuals across teams, departments, companies, and industries whom you select with purpose, engage consistently, and nurture with care. This isn't casual networking. It's strategic relationship stewardship. Where traditional networks grow by chance, your Power Circle grows by choice, aligned with your goals and guided by your mission.

Why a Power Circle Is Different

A Power Circle is built on strategic value, not social comfort. It's fueled by consistent interaction, not once-a-year check-ins. It's composed of diverse, high-impact roles: mentors, sponsors, connectors, challengers, and more. And it is proactively maintained through regular check-ins, timely updates, and purposeful engagement.

Success doesn't just come from what you do. It comes from who knows what you do, who advocates for your advancement, and who opens doors you didn't even know existed. Your Power Circle becomes your reputation amplifier, opportunity engine, emotional firewall, and career insurance policy. It's a strategic support system that works for you even when you're not in the room

Introduction to Power Circles

In every workplace, power is not just about titles or hierarchy, it's about influence, access, and perception. If you're serious about advancing your goals while navigating complex power dynamics, you need more than just a mentor. You need a strategy. This is where the Power Circles method comes in.

Power Circles is a strategic tool that helps you map and manage the relationships that either advance or obstruct your success. It forces clarity around who truly supports you, who stays neutral, and who may be quietly undermining you. It also helps you identify those with indirect influence, people who don't control your destiny directly, but shape what the real power holders think about you.

This method gives you a repeatable way to assess, map, and act based on visually coded behavioral traits. It ensures you're not just hoping relationships work in your favor. You're actively managing them to serve your goals.

Not everyone belongs in your Power Circle. You need a method of evaluating, prioritizing and screening those who belong in your

Power Circle, those who can help you to achieve your goals while filtering out those who block their attainment.

The Five Steps of the Power Circle Methodology

Step 1: Define Your Goal

Before navigating any relationships, be clear: What is your professional objective? Are you aiming for a promotion, a high-profile project, or visibility with senior leadership? Your Power Circle should be built around that specific goal. Every person you evaluate is assessed based on whether they help or hinder that goal.

Step 2: Gather or create an organization chart or diagram that you will use to identify the key players that can help or hinder you attaining that goal.

These tools reflect both the individual and reporting relationships in the organization. This illuminates two features: official reporting relationships and communication webs. In other words, you can visualize how messages might travel between contacts. Sources of this data include organization charts, project rosters, team documentation, or information you can get from key administrative assistants who have the best visibility into how different employees relate to each other.

As you build your chart, think beyond direct supervisors. Include stakeholders, decision-makers, support roles, cross-functional partners, peers and informal influencers. Also don't limit yourself to just inside your immediate organization. Look sideways. Every manager or executive has a peer that they respect and who wield considerable power to shape perceptions about you. At this stage the goal is just to compile a list of potential players regardless of whether they ultimately help or hinder you. That insight will emerge during analysis in the following steps.

To illustrate this method, we'll use the fictional company **ACME Marketing** to show how the Power Circle method transforms everyday contacts into a strategic force for career advancement as shown in **Figure A**. which depicts each colleague, their reporting relationship and role/title.

ACME Marketing Company

Figure A. Org Chart

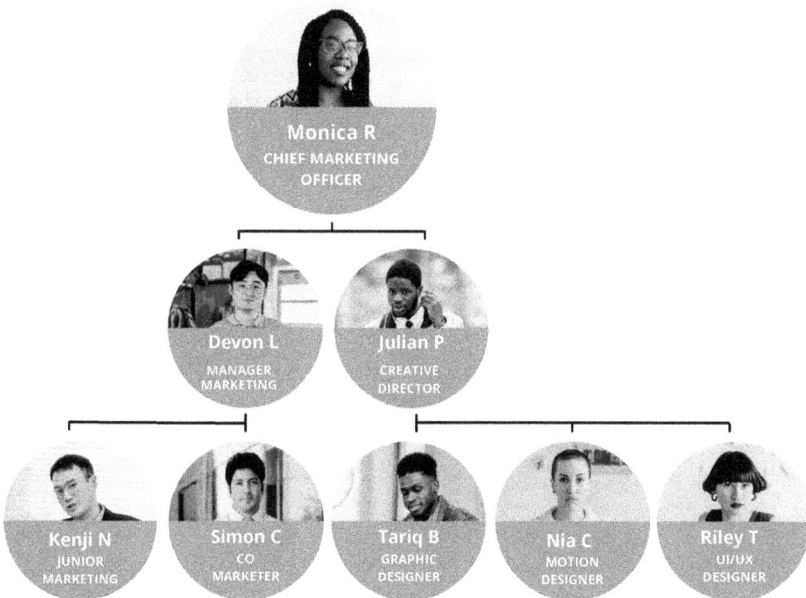

Step 3: Categorize Individuals by Their Alignment With Your Goal

With your org chart ready, assign each person a symbol or a color code based on their behavior. Ask yourself: Are they advancing your goals or standing in the way? Have they demonstrated inclination towards supporting you with others or are they an unknown? Your answer will place each person into one of the following categories:

- **ADVOCATES** are coded as **STARS** ★ (or the color Green). These are loyal and outspoken supporters. They also act as strategic connectors who can link you to people or resources that help move your goals forward.
- **POTENTIAL ALLIES** are coded as a **PLUS "+"** (or the color Blue). They are respectful but untested individuals who show signs of support but haven't yet acted. They give the right vibes to become an Advocate but need nurturing.
- **NEUTRALS** are coded as a **QUESTION MARK " ? "** (or the color Yellow). Neutrals don't give a sense of where they stand yet. They are passive, unclear contacts whose position or intentions remain undefined.
- **DETRACTORS** are coded as a **MINUS "—"** (or the color Red). Detractors are those who consistently block, devalue, or undermine your efforts.

As you can see, by adding symbols or color to reflect advocacy towards you, you get an immediate visual understanding of the power landscape as it relates to the attainment of your goals. Now you can visually "see" where help is likely to come from or anticipated attacks (Figure B).

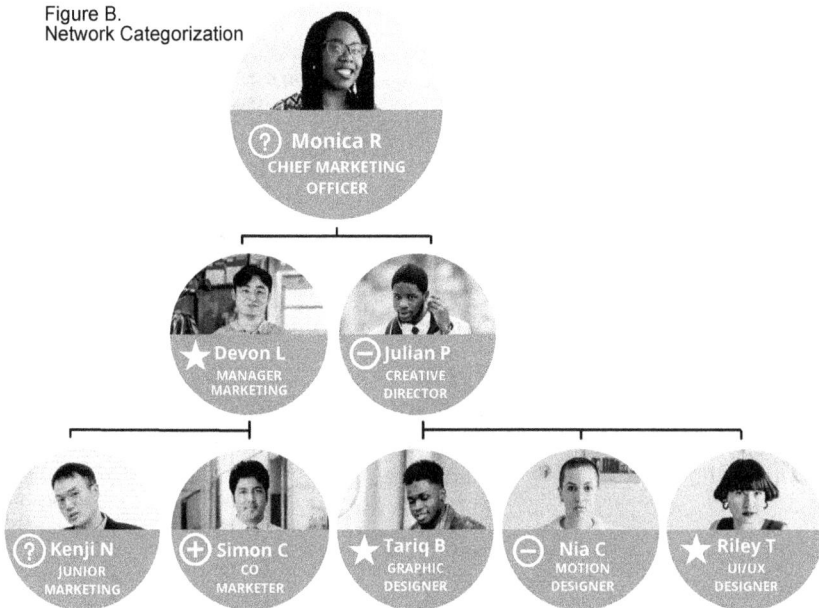

Figure B.
Network Categorization

Step 4: Rate the Degree of Influence Each Person Has

Knowing whether each person is aligned with you is not enough. You also need to know what degree of INFLUENCE each person has to put actions into effect. A person that advocates for you but has no influence has no ability to move you towards your goal. By understanding this you know where to focus your engagement and energy. The degree of influence a person has translates into the level of effort and engagement strategy you deploy.

You last used symbols or color codes to denote advocacy. Now you will map an influence score for each person. Place a number "1" on each contact that has a low perceived level of influence, a "2" for medium and "3" for the highest level of influence. Each person should now have two codes to denote advocacy and influence as depicted in Figure C.

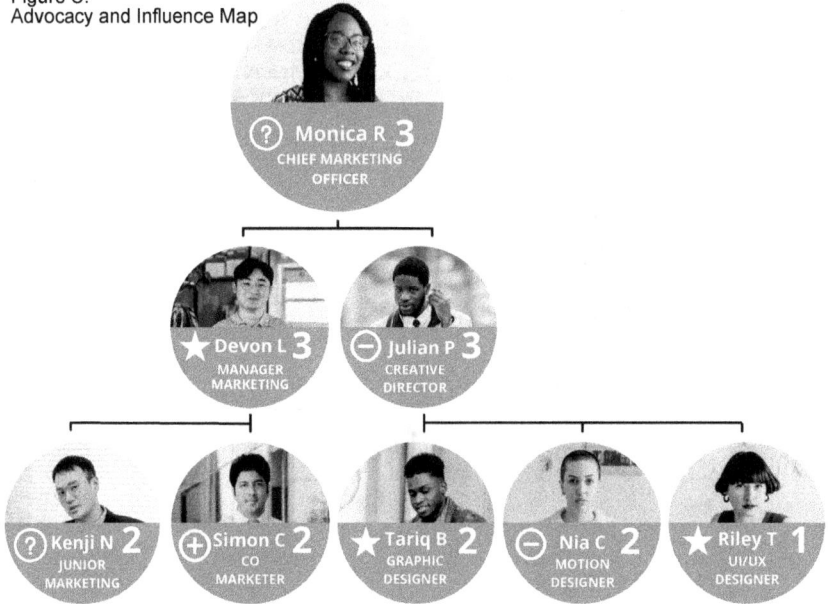

Figure C.
Advocacy and Influence Map

The degree of influence each contact has combined with their respective advocacy code (the symbol or color code) determines the engagement strategy to deploy that we'll cover next.

Step 5. Determine the Engagement Strategy for Each Contact

Advocates (★/GREEN)

Advocates are people you trust with your best interests (as they trust you). You want to deepen the relationship, build closer ties, and grow a mutually beneficial business relationship.

Devon, Tariq, and Riley each have positive relationships with Monica. Devon was promoted as a manager under Monica's tutelage and has the highest level of influence with Monica. Tariq and Riley were hired by Monica. Both have lesser degrees of influence though they have great relationships with Monica. Both are growing in their careers, have key connections and have demonstrated strong advocacy of you to others. You will want to continue to grow and deepen your connections with them. For each of the three Advocates, this can mean catching up on the latest interests that one might have, going to coffee or tea shops on breaks with another, or informal routine check-ins.

Potential Allies (✚/BLUE)

Potential Allies are promising but unproven. They exhibit friendliness, occasional collaboration, or moments of encouragement. However, they haven't yet demonstrated consistent support or direct advocacy.

With Potential Allies, your strategic goal is to *test and cultivate*. These are not people to flood with personal information or high-stakes expectations right away. Instead, create low-risk, high-value interactions that give them space to show where they stand. Invite them into shared wins like small collaborations, informal brainstorming sessions, or mutual support moments where both of you can benefit.

Your strategy here is consistency without overcommitment. Look for signs of reciprocation. If after multiple touchpoints they begin to ask about your goals, offer help, or include you in new opportunities, they're ripening into Advocates. Move them closer.

Neutrals (? /YELLOW)

Neutrals are hardest to read and the most dangerous to ignore. Their silence may be genuine detachment, quiet observation, or passive resistance. Their influence ranges widely, but their behavior lacks clarity. You're unsure if they're allies in waiting or silent obstacles.

With Neutrals, your strategic move is to probe and clarify. Start by evaluating whether their neutrality is due to lack of exposure to your work, lack of interest, or deliberate disconnection. Your next steps depend on that insight.

Neutrals should not be ignored or written off. Some are silent influencers. Others are fence-sitters who follow the dominant voices. If you stay invisible to them, you risk becoming irrelevant or vulnerable to narratives you can't control. Illuminate their role and direction. If you sense curiosity or appreciation for your work, start nudging the relationship forward. If you sense apathy or quiet dismissal, deprioritize, but continue to monitor.

Detractors (➖/RED)

Detractors are not always overt. In fact, many operate subtly. They block your efforts behind closed doors and dismiss your contributions in meetings. They also consistently withhold support others receive freely. They may feel threatened by your presence, indifferent to your goals, or fueled by personal bias.

With Detractors, your strategy is to neutralize, outmaneuver, or contain.

Do not waste energy trying to win their affection. Your time is better spent protecting your reputation, minimizing their ability to interfere, and building insulation through your Advocates and sponsors.

When facing Detractors with high influence, elevate your professionalism. Be measured. Be direct when necessary. Use facts and visibility to disarm misperceptions. And most critically: expand the circle of people who see your value firsthand so Detractors cannot define your narrative.

ENGAGEMENT STRATEGIES

The following table outlines a set of engagement strategies based on two key dimensions: an individual's support type and their influence level. It provides guidance on how to interact with advocates, potential allies, neutral parties, and detractors in ways that strengthen relationships, manage risks, and optimize outcomes. The strategies scale from high- to low-influence individuals to help tailor your approach effectively.

Figure D. Engagement Strategy Table

SUPPORT TYPE

INFLUENCE LEVEL	★ ADVOCATE	⊕ POTENTIAL ALLY	? NEUTRAL	⊖ DETRACTOR
High (3)	Put them in the spotlight and align their visibility with yours to elevate both of your power.	Engage them directly—invite them into high-level conversations to test loyalty and convert them.	Watch closely—build rapport subtly while observing their patterns of influence.	Neutralize them through structure—limit their access and build alliances that dilute their reach.
Medium (2)	Keep them engaged with selective inclusion in strategy so they remain invested and vocal in your favor.	Build trust by looping them into wins and sharing limited access—they need nudging to fully commit.	Maintain consistent but surface-level contact; avoid oversharing or assuming alignment.	Don't provoke—disarm with professionalism and gather support around them to reduce their impact.
Low (1)	Affirm their loyalty with appreciation, but don't over-invest—keep it lightweight and supportive.	Offer encouragement and small ways to participate; assess if they're worth cultivating.	Keep interactions minimal and courteous—they hold little power but can influence perceptions.	Stay polite, but disengaged—don't feed drama or let them distract from more important players.

Now that you've mapped out your workplace network, you've turned abstract workplace dynamics into a living, breathing strategy. This exercise isn't just about identifying who's around you. It's about clarifying who truly moves the needle, influences perceptions, and helps (or hinders) your goals. Seeing your network visually allows you to be intentional about where you invest your time, how you build alliances, and where hidden opportunities for influence may lie.

These strategic tools represent more than roles and titles. It's a snapshot of power in motion. The below graphic represents an evolving Power Circle made up of trusted, vetted advocates that are part of your inner circle Figure E. As your relationships evolve, so should your inner circle and those on its periphery. Update it regularly, track who's gaining influence, and be strategic about how you show up in those relationships. When managed with clarity and intention, your Power Circle becomes one of the most valuable assets in your career— one that fuels your visibility, multiplies your impact, and protects your path to advancement.

Figure E. My Power Circle

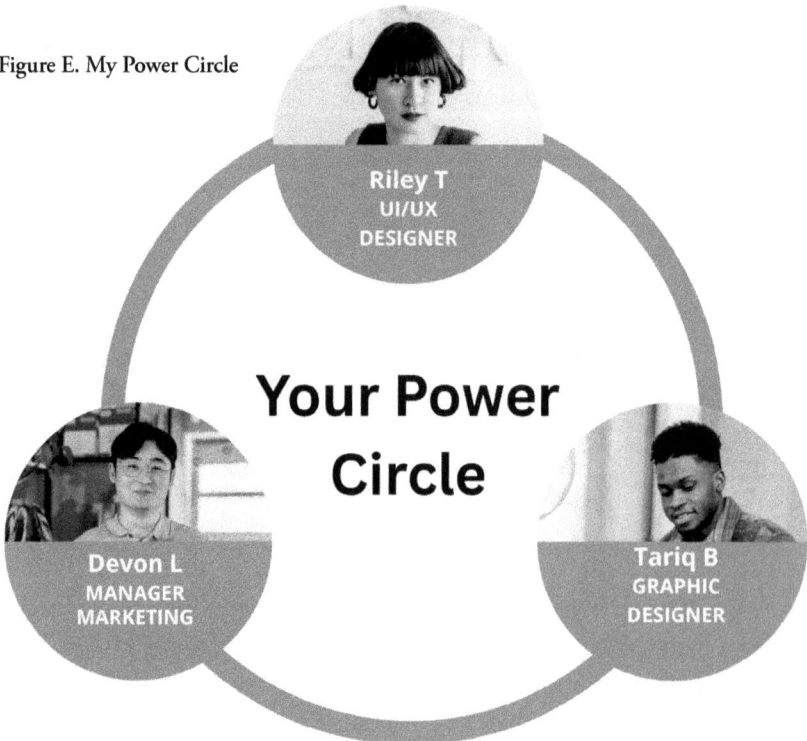

Riley T
UI/UX
DESIGNER

Your Power
Circle

Devon L
MANAGER
MARKETING

Tariq B
GRAPHIC
DESIGNER

Case Study: The Detractor She Saw Coming

Alyssa had been in her role less than a year when she was tapped as a potential candidate for a Director-level promotion. Her project had exceeded every goal, and leaders were starting to take notice. But Alyssa had done more than deliver results. She had mapped her Power Ecosystem.

That's how she spotted Marla.

Marla was a Senior Director in another division. They didn't work closely, but Alyssa noticed the negative vibes from her early: dismissive comments in meetings, subtle undermining, and a backhanded remark to a VP that Alyssa might "need a few more years" to grow.

Instead of reacting, Alyssa got strategic.

She strengthened her Power Circle by meeting regularly with Marla's boss, updating her sponsor, and building allies inside Marla's team. She made sure her work and leadership style were visible to the people who mattered, before anything could be weaponized against her.

Sure enough, just before decisions were finalized for the promotion, Marla quietly raised "concerns" about Alyssa's readiness to step into the new role.

But the attack didn't land.

Her sponsor had already advocated for her. Her reputation was documented and reinforced. The leadership team had already bought in thanks to Alyssa's powerplay! Alyssa got the promotion and Marla's move backfired quietly.

Takeaway: Alyssa didn't wait for the attack to defend herself. She positioned herself so well that the threat collapsed on arrival. That's what happens when you use your Power Circle before the game is played.

Part III

Personas & Personalities

♀

HOW TO DECODE YOUR COLLEAGUES: 11 PERSONAS THAT CONTROL EVERY WORKPLACE

Walk into any office believing everyone plays fair, and you'll miss what's actually happening. People don't leave their fears, ambitions, and protective instincts at home. They bring them into every meeting, every email, every conversation. And if you're a woman, you won't just navigate male-dominated spaces; you'll work alongside other women who've already developed their own survival blueprints.

This guide decodes the behavioral patterns that emerge when advancement feels scarce, recognition requires fighting for, and office politics operate below the waterline. These aren't stereotypes. They're real composites shaped by workplace pressure, learned caution, strategic thinking, and sometimes desperation.

Recognizing these patterns helps you:

- Identify behaviors that quietly erode your credibility
- Decode hidden agendas and their underlying fears
- Catch yourself falling into similar traps
- Develop sharper professional instincts

When Survival Tactics Become Second Nature

Take Rachel, a project lead who started noticing contradictions everywhere. Her supposed mentor praised her privately but never mentioned Rachel's contributions in executive rooms. A peer acted like her biggest supporter yet somehow always positioned herself at the center of team successes. Meanwhile, Rachel kept silent during high-stakes presentations, choosing comfort over career momentum.

None of this reflected poor character. These were defense mechanisms built over time in environments where women believed they had to pick between being well-liked and being taken seriously. Rachel's mentor had internalized that championing other women made male executives question her judgment. Her peer had learned that in workplaces where credit disappears quickly, you grab it first or lose it forever. Rachel herself had absorbed the belief that keeping peace outweighed advocating for herself.

The Systems That Shape Behavior

These personas endure because organizational structures breed scarcity thinking, particularly for women. When there's an invisible quota of "one successful woman per team," or when assertiveness has historically triggered punishment, people adapt. Some become excessively agreeable to dodge the "difficult" label. Others turn ruthlessly competitive because the system demands it. Most switch strategies based on how much pressure they're under.

Your edge comes from understanding these patterns aren't about you. When coworkers push back against your proposals, they're often protecting themselves from being ignored again rather than critiquing your actual work. When someone withholds support, they might be avoiding professional fallout you haven't experienced yet.

Once you see these dynamics as calculated responses to flawed systems rather than personality defects, you can navigate them strategically. You can create paper trails that let cautious colleagues back your ideas safely. You can develop countermeasures for people skilled at claiming credit. Most crucially, you can practice constructive conflict, learning that thoughtful pushback usually strengthens professional relationships instead of destroying them.

What This Guide Gives You

The eleven personas that follow capture widespread behavioral patterns across industries. Each profile helps you spot these types quickly, grasp what drives them, and choose smart engagement tactics. Just as importantly, each includes reflection prompts to catch yourself slipping into these same patterns, plus actionable steps for change.

Keep this in mind: these personas aren't fixed identities nor are they mutually exclusive. They're flexible responses that shift as people and workplaces evolve. Your mission isn't judging others but building the emotional intelligence that lets you succeed regardless of who's in the room.

THE HUMBLE HELPER

They're the one everyone turns to. The reliable problem solver. The "get it done" teammate. They're helpful, hardworking, and selfless. But they stay quiet, avoid attention, and rarely speak up to showcase their value.

Strengths:

- Consistent, trustworthy, and team-oriented
- Builds strong peer relationships
- Willing to go above and beyond

Weaknesses:

- They assume that hard work alone will speak for itself. But in many workplaces, visibility is just as important as output. Because they avoid attention and rarely share their wins, their contributions are often taken for granted or claimed by others.
- They quietly carry the load while louder colleagues take the credit. This dynamic can leave them stuck in supportive roles, even if they're doing leadership-level work

Self-Reflection: How to know if this is you

If others are getting promoted for work you helped drive or your name is rarely mentioned in rooms where decisions are made. It is a sign that being essential behind the scenes is not the same as being seen.

Ask yourself:

- Do I believe that asking for credit makes me seem self-centered?
- Do I feel awkward owning my success (even when it's earned)?
- Am I more comfortable supporting others than leading openly?

Start by noticing when you shrink from the spotlight, especially when you've earned it.

Real-World Scenario

You lead a project from the ground up solving problems, managing details, and keeping everything on track. At the final presentation, a teammate volunteers to present. You agree. They get the credit. You stay invisible. Again.

What to Do Instead:

- Pair helpfulness with leadership. Ask to be the one presenting team work.
- Set boundaries so you're not always the fallback.
- Document and share results clearly in emails or debriefs.
- Practice how to say: "Here's what I contributed and how it helped"

How to Recover

It's not too late to reclaim your voice. After a project wraps, follow up: "I appreciated the team's work on this. Here's what I focused on and the results we achieved."

You don't have to call anyone out. Just call yourself forward.

Empowerment Reminder:

Being generous is a strength. Being invisible is not. You can support others and still advocate for yourself.

How to Navigate This Persona (if it's a colleague)

The Humble Helper is motivated by a deep sense of responsibility, loyalty, and a desire to be seen as dependable. They often avoid the spotlight, even when their contributions are critical.

To work effectively with them, acknowledge their strengths genuinely and give them space to share their insights without pressure. They respond best to trust and inclusion, not competition. Invite them into strategic conversations by asking for their perspective; they often have a clear understanding of behind-the-scenes dynamics, even if they hesitate to speak up. By recognizing their quietly earned credibility, you not only build a stronger partnership, you also tap into a powerful but underutilized ally. They are more likely to champion your efforts, offer support, and strengthen team outcomes when they feel seen, valued, and safe.

Leading with respect earns their trust and that trust can become a stable foundation for shared success.

THE HARMONY KEEPER

They're polite, peace-loving, and rarely push back. They avoid confrontation, let others talk over them, and back down when challenged. Their goal is to keep the peace, but that silence comes at a cost. They often believe that speaking up will damage relationships, make them appear difficult, or lead to tension they'd rather avoid. But in protecting others' comfort, they sacrifice their own credibility. Over time, their silence becomes a pattern others learn to expect.

Strengths:

- Seen as kind, calm, and easy to work with
- Avoids unnecessary friction
- Adaptable in group setting

Weaknesses:

Their fear of conflict makes them hesitant to assert ideas or challenge group decisions. But by avoiding healthy disagreement, they unintentionally give others silent permission to:

- Dismiss their input
- Claim credit for their work
- Make decisions without their voice

Self-Reflection: How to know if this is you

If you leave meetings feeling unheard, or notice others taking credit for your ideas while you stay quiet, it's time to raise your voice (professionally). Ask yourself:

- Do I stay silent because I fear being seen as aggressive?
- Do I replay meetings in my head, wishing I'd spoken up?
- Do I equate disagreement with conflict or disapproval?

Pay attention to the moments when you hold yourself back from speaking up or asserting your value, even when your perspective and contribution matter.

Real-World Scenario

In a team meeting, a colleague suggests a direction you believe won't work. You disagree internally but say nothing. Later, when the plan fails, you realize you could've changed the outcome but you feared seeming "negative" or "difficult."

What to Do Instead:

- Practice calm disagreement: "I respect that view, but here's another angle."
- Follow up on contributions in writing: "As discussed, here's the idea I raised…"
- Rehearse responses to pushback so you're not caught off guard. Learn to say: "I hear what you are saying, but I see it differently, and here's why."
- Protect your ideas by putting them in writing or speaking up early.

How to Recover

It's okay to circle back. Try: "I've been thinking more about our earlier conversation and wanted to share my full perspective now that I've had time to reflect." This not only protects your ideas, it shows maturity, clarity, and strategic presence.

Empowerment Reminder:

Your perspective matters. When you speak up, others learn how to treat you. Don't trade your voice for short-term comfort.

How to Navigate This Persona
(if it's a colleague)

The Harmony Keeper values harmony and emotional safety. To connect with her, create low-pressure, one-on-one spaces where she feels safe to share honestly. She's more likely to speak when she trusts she won't face judgment or backlash.

Build trust by respecting her boundaries and allowing time to reflect. Though quiet in the moment, she often notices what others miss. When she feels seen and supported, she becomes a loyal, steady ally who adds calm clarity to group decisions.

Invite her in gently and follow up. Her voice, once welcomed, can shift the room.

THE APPROVAL SEEKER

They're warm, well-liked, and focused on keeping everyone comfortable, even at their own expense. The Approval Seeker goes out of their way to avoid conflict, smooth over tension, and be seen as agreeable. But in trying to keep the peace, they often lose their voice. They avoid hard conversations, water down feedback, and hesitate to advocate for themselves when it might make others uncomfortable.

Strengths:

- Kind, approachable, and easy to work with
- Creates emotional safety in teams
- Skilled at defusing tension and promoting harmony

Weaknesses:

- Struggles to assert needs or boundaries
- Avoids healthy conflict, leading to miscommunication or resentment
- May appear agreeable but feel overlooked or unheard

Self-Reflection: How to know if this is you

You may identify with this persona if you:

- Say yes even when you want to say no
- Avoid giving honest feedback to keep others happy

- Feel responsible for making sure no one's upset, even when it's not your burden

Real-World Scenario

You're asked to stay late to help with a project yet again. You say yes, even though you're overwhelmed. You don't push back or share that you're drowning. Later, when someone else gets praised for the project's success, you quietly wonder why your extra effort didn't count.

What to Do Instead:

- Pair helpfulness with leadership. Ask to be the one presenting team work.
- Set boundaries so you're not always the fallback.
- Document and share results clearly in emails or debriefs.
- Practice how to say: "Here's what I contributed and how it helped"

How to Recover

If you've already said yes too many times, try a reset: "I've realized I've taken on more than I can handle. I want to be helpful, but I'll need to step back from this one."

How to Navigate This Persona (if it's a colleague)

The Approval Seeker will rarely push back or claim credit, even when they deserve it. If you need something from them, be respectful and direct. They may avoid hard truths, but they value fairness and trust.

Support them by creating space for them to voice their thoughts privately. If they hesitate to speak in meetings, follow up one-on-one: "I noticed you didn't get to weigh in earlier. What's your take?"

By treating them as someone whose opinion matters, not just someone who smooths things over, you create conditions for a stronger working relationship. They'll be more open with you when they see that your respect for them doesn't depend on their being agreeable.

THE EMPATHY SPONGE

Empathetic and emotionally attuned, the Empathy Sponge has a natural instinct to support others. They notice when someone's struggling and often step in to offer comfort or help. But in the workplace, this can become a burden. They carry others' emotions as if they're their own, prioritize feelings over facts, and sometimes lose sight of professional boundaries. Their compassion is real, but when unmanaged, it can drain their energy and reduce their influence.

Strengths:

- Highly empathetic and emotionally intelligent
- Creates psychological safety and emotional trust
- Often the first to notice when someone needs support

Weaknesses:

- Can become overly involved in others' emotional experiences
- May avoid difficult decisions to protect others' feelings
- Risks being perceived as soft or overly sensitive

Self-Reflection: How to know if this is you

You may identify with this persona if you:

- Absorb others' stress and carry it with you

- Feel responsible for managing how others feel even when it's not your role
- Constantly prioritize harmony, even when it hurts productivity

Real-World Scenario

A coworker vents to you about how overwhelmed they feel. Instead of redirecting or offering perspective, you take it on staying late to help with their workload and emotionally carrying their stress. Later, when your own work slips, no one realizes why.

What to Do Instead:

- Offer empathy without over-involving yourself: "That sounds hard. What do you think you'll do?"
- Protect your time and energy before rescuing others
- Prioritize solutions over emotional bonding in high-stress moments
- Set emotional boundaries while still being supportive

How to Recover

If you've overextended emotionally, acknowledge it and pivot: "I want to be supportive, but I've realized I need to focus on my responsibilities too. Let's figure out what resources might help you."

How to Navigate This Persona (if it's a colleague)

The Empathy Sponge is often the one checking in, offering to help, or absorbing others' stress. If you're working with someone like this, appreciate their support, but don't offload your stress onto them. Be mindful of how much emotional labor you're asking them to carry, and consider whether you're treating them as a colleague or as an informal therapist.

If you need to redirect them, do so with kindness: "I really value your support. Can I get your thoughts on this strategy?" This helps them feel useful without being emotionally overwhelmed. You'll build trust by showing you respect both their heart and their mind.

When working with an Empathy Sponge, also watch for signs that they're overextending themselves. If you notice them taking on more than their share or seeming unusually stressed, check in with them directly. Sometimes they need permission to prioritize their own needs, and a simple "How are you holding up?" can remind them that their wellbeing matters too.

Finally, when they do offer support, be specific about what would actually be helpful. Instead of general venting, try asking for specific advice, resources, or perspective. This helps them feel useful while channeling their desire to help in more productive directions.

THE CHEERLEADER

Warm, affirming, and endlessly encouraging, the Cheerleader thrives on positivity. They lift spirits, celebrate others, and work hard to keep morale high. But their constant reassurance can come at a cost. In trying to protect feelings and preserve harmony, they hesitate to offer honest feedback or express disagreement. Their support is genuine, yet their avoidance of discomfort can make their praise feel safe but shallow.

Strengths:

- Supportive, empathetic, and emotionally intuitive
- Great at building safe team dynamics and morale
- Seen as approachable and easy to work with
- Quickly picks up on group energy and relational tension

Weaknesses:

- Avoids hard truths or critical conversations
- Praises others indiscriminately, reducing credibility
- Rarely offers dissenting views in meetings
- Prioritizes being liked over being clear or effective

Self-Reflection: How to know if this is you

You might identify with this persona if:

- You give positive feedback even when it's not fully earned
- You worry that disagreement will damage the relationship
- You often replay conversations, wondering if you were too harsh, even when you were soft
- You keep your critiques to yourself and offer encouragement instead

Real-World Scenario

Your colleague delivers a presentation that misses the mark. It is confusing, unstructured, and off target. Afterward, they ask what you thought. You smile and say, "I think you handled it well. It's a tough topic." Later, they're surprised when leadership questions their logic. They assumed they did fine because you said so. They feel misled. And you feel complicit.

By sparing their feelings, you cost them credibility. And in doing so, you weakened your own.

What to Do Instead:

Be clear and kind—not just kind. Say: "You're great under pressure, but I think the structure needed work. Want help brainstorming next time?"

- Offer honesty with support: praise what worked and name what didn't
- Practice disagreement that doesn't damage relationships
- Know that people respect truth even if they flinch at first
- Your power grows when your encouragement is earned, not automatic.

How to Recover

Begin small. Next time someone asks for your feedback, pause before defaulting to praise. Choose one honest point they can grow from. Then say it gently but clearly. If you've built a reputation as "nice but vague," reset by offering clarity in places people don't expect. You'll stand out and eventually be sought out. People can find cheerleaders anywhere. They look for advisors in truth-tellers.

How to Navigate This Persona (if it's a colleague)

The Cheerleader is uplifting and well-meaning, but they may offer encouragement over accuracy. Appreciate their warmth, but don't rely on them for critical calibration. To work well with them:

- Ask for specifics when they praise you: "What part stood out to you most?"
- Don't mistake their compliments for full validation. Seek a second opinion if stakes are high
- Invite them into feedback moments by making them low-risk
- Give them space to be honest: "You're always supportive. I'd love to hear the truth, even if it's tough."

THE SILENT CALCULATOR

Quiet but never checked out, the Silent Calculator is always running the numbers in their head. It's just not the financial kind. They're reading the room, weighing outcomes, and deciding when to play their cards. They let others talk, reveal their opinions, and take the heat while they gather data. Every silence is intentional, every word calculated. To some, they seem mysterious or detached. In reality, they're just two steps ahead: observing, positioning, and waiting for the exact right moment to move.

Every move they make is measured. Every silence, every contribution, every alignment is intentional. They know the risks of over-exposure and avoid premature opinions. Colleagues may call them mysterious or aloof. But behind the scenes, they're reading power dynamics with precision.

Strengths:

- Highly observant, strategic, and emotionally intelligent
- Excellent at reading agendas, alliances, and motives
- Speaks only when it matters. Her words carry weight
- Rarely gets dragged into drama or missteps publicly

Weaknesses:

- Comes across as distant, guarded, or hard to read
- Can be overlooked in fast-moving discussions
- Struggles to build trust if others feel shut out
- May miss opportunities by waiting too long to act

Self-Reflection: How to know if this is you

You might be this persona if:

- You're always the last to speak (if you speak at all)
- You second-guess how people will perceive your input
- You're cautious to the point of invisibility
- You only contribute when you're 100% confident

Real-World Scenario

In a team meeting, people go back and forth about which way to go. You spot the problem right away but decide to sit on it. You think it through and stay quiet. Leadership moves ahead anyway.

The plan runs into major challenges just like you thought it would. Later they ask why you didn't say anything. You shrug and say you didn't want to step on toes.

But that pause cost you. Thinking it over did not help. It kept you from steering the decision and being seen as someone who leads, not just someone who watches.

What to Do Instead:

- Speak earlier, even if it's measured: "I've been thinking through this. Here's one concern I have…"
- Share what you notice, not just what's safe
- Ask strategic questions that guide direction
- Use your insights to influence, not just observe

How to Recover

Start by shifting your ratio: instead of 90% listening and 10% speaking, aim for 70/30. Choose one meeting to offer your POV early, even if it's just a framing question. Follow up in writing if you hesitate in real-time: "Wanted to add something I didn't get to say earlier…" With time, people will associate your voice with insight, not silence. Strategic thinkers get credit *when they speak* not just when they're right in hindsight.

Empowerment Reminder:

Your silence isn't wrong. But it can't do the talking for you. When you pair discernment with courage, people stop guessing and start listening.

How to Navigate This Persona (if it's a colleague)

The Silent Calculator is highly strategic but doesn't always let others in. Don't misinterpret their restraint as lack of insight. They're watching everything and probably knows more than they say. To work well with them:

- Give them space to think but invite them in directly: "I'd really value your take on this, what's your read?"
- Don't pressure them to be vocal. Ask questions that draw them out

THE VIPER

The Viper is charming and well-connected, thriving in social settings and building strong relationships with leadership. But they use this influence strategically. They praise people publicly while subtly undermining them privately. They don't engage in overt sabotage, but slowly erode competitors' credibility through calculated comments. Their social standing protects them from being called out, but their behavior creates toxic dynamics that fracture team trust over time.

Strengths

- Socially adept and highly likable
- Skilled at relationship-building with leadership
- Influential in informal power circles
- Perceived as confident, witty, and engaging

Weaknesses

- Uses charm to mask insecurity or power plays
- May manipulate perception to elevate herself
- Erodes team trust by planting doubt
- Avoids direct confrontation but excels at passive sabotage

Self-Reflection: How to Know If This Is You

You might be this persona if:

- You praise people in public but criticize them in private settings
- You feel threatened when others are recognized or promoted
- You offer compliments that also serve as digs
- You quietly position yourself as the more capable one in casual conversations

Ask yourself:

- Do I build others up as much as I build myself up?
- Am I motivated by influence or insecurity?
- Would I speak the same way if the person were in the room?

Influence without integrity always shows itself eventually. Better to be known for what you contribute, not what you chip away.

Real-World Scenario

Your teammate is selected to present to senior leadership. You smile and say, "That's great!" but in a separate chat, you message another colleague:

"Interesting choice. I thought they struggled with the last project." Word gets around. The person hears about it. Trust is broken. Your public praise is no longer believable, and you're seen as two-faced. Suddenly, people keep their distance. And it's not because you aren't liked, but because they can't tell what's real.

What to Do Instead

- Celebrate others without adding qualifiers
- If you have feedback, give it directly, not through backchannels
- Focus on collaboration, not competition
- Use your social influence to elevate not isolate

Leadership notices who builds teams. Not just who builds buzz.

How to Recover

If you've been called out or exposed, apologize directly:

"I regret what I said. It wasn't fair and it didn't reflect how I want to show up." Then change your habits. Practice speaking well of people even when they are not around. Align your private voice with your public one. Trust will return slowly and surely.

How to Navigate This Persona (if it's a colleague)

The Viper can be intimidating. They are well-connected and highly visible. But you don't need to compete with them on their terms.

Document your work and contributions consistently

- Don't engage in gossip. Stay neutral and professional
- Set boundaries: "I'd prefer we address this directly with them."
- Build your own allies who see your value clearly

Their influence can't harm you if your credibility is clear, consistent, and rooted in integrity.

THE BENEDICT ARNOLD

The Benedict Arnold is the type who appears supportive, until support requires risk or sacrifice. They're warm in public, agreeable in meetings, and might even co-sign your ideas when there's no heat involved. But when conflict arises or visibility shifts, they vanish. Or worse, they align themselves with whoever holds the most power in that moment.

Strengths

- Politically astute and tuned in to power dynamics
- Often seen as agreeable and non-confrontational
- Quick to adapt and align with majority decisions
- Maintains positive relationships with influential players

Weaknesses

- Avoids backing colleagues when it could cost them something
- Withholds support during tension or controversy
- Perceived as unreliable or disloyal by peers
- Prioritizes safety over principle or consistency

Self-Reflection: How to Know If This Is You

You might relate to this persona if:

- You support people privately but stay silent when they're challenged
- You've shifted positions based on who was in the room
- You withhold opinions until you know where leadership stands
- You use neutrality as a shield, even when stakes are high

Ask yourself:

- Do I show up only when it's easy?
- What would it look like to back someone (even when it's risky)?
- Am I protecting myself at the cost of someone else's credibility?

Being strategic isn't the same as being silent. True allies show up even when it's inconvenient.

Real-World Scenario

You agree with a peer's idea in a private chat, even help shape it. But in a team meeting, when it's challenged by leadership, you stay quiet. Or worse, pivot entirely, saying: "I see the concern, too."

Your colleague is left exposed, and others notice the shift. The trust you had is eroded. Later, when you need backup, no one steps up. Why? Because support, like loyalty, is earned both ways.

What to Do Instead:

- Speak up when it counts, not just when it's safe
- Say: "I think there's value here. Let's explore it further"

- Take small, consistent risks to build trust
- Don't co-sign in private what you won't defend in public
- Allyship is an action, not a whisper. Show people they can count on you.

How to Recover

If you've let someone down by disappearing at the wrong moment, start here: "I realized I stayed quiet when I should've spoken up. That wasn't fair to you. I'm working on being a more consistent supporter." Then do it. Support out loud. Align your private values with your public actions.

How to Navigate This Persona (if it's a colleague)

The Benedict Arnold can seem like a friend, until they're not. Don't over- invest emotionally if they're only present when it benefits them.

- Test consistency before assuming loyalty
- Get commitments in writing when collaboration matters
- Don't rely on them during politically sensitive situations
- Protect your credibility independently

They'll float with power. You stay anchored in principle and others will follow your example.

THE WORKHORSE

They're the early arriver, the late stayer, the one who never misses a deadline and always goes above and beyond. Their motto? 'If I work hard enough, I'll get noticed.' And they do get noticed for their effort. But not always for their leadership. They're dependable, diligent, and humble. But in their push to prove themselves, they often forget to show what they're capable of beyond the task list. Their dedication becomes their reputation, but not their leverage.

Strengths:

- Exceptionally reliable and results-driven
- Sets a high bar for quality and execution
- Trusted with critical tasks and consistent follow-through

Weaknesses:

- Equates effort with advancement, without building strategic relationships
- Stays buried in the work while others get visibility
- Avoids advocating for herself or highlighting her leadership potential

Self-Reflection: How to know if this is you

You might be this persona if you:

- Feel pride in being the most dependable person on the team
- Avoid speaking up about your contributions, hoping others will notice
- Rarely step back to connect with mentors or decision-makers

Real-World Scenario

You stay late to triple-check the numbers, polish the deck, and prep the meeting room. Everything goes smoothly. However, your manager gets the praise. You're thanked in passing, but no one knows how much you handled behind the scenes.

What to Do Instead:

- Share your contributions clearly: "Here's what I handled for today's prep."
- Ask to lead small components, not just support them
- Schedule checkins with mentors, not just managers
- Use visibility as a strategy not a reward

How to Recover

If you've stayed behind the scenes too long, start by following up after moments where your work showed up but your name didn't. Try: "Glad that went smoothly. Just to recap, I handled the budget check, visuals, and logistics."

How to Navigate This Persona
(if it's a colleague)

The Workhorse can be a valuable ally if you know how to work with them. They're task-focused, detail-oriented, and thrive on structure. They may not offer unsolicited advice or mentorship, but they notice who's dependable, respectful, and sharp.

Build trust by being prepared, showing initiative, and respecting their time. When you step up thoughtfully, they're more likely to see you as competent and include you in key tasks or problem-solving moments.

If they're taking on too much, offer to share part of the workload. But do it in a way that reinforces their leadership: "You've got a lot going on. Want me to run with this part so you can focus on the bigger pieces?"

This shows that you're not trying to compete, you're reinforcing their position while gaining visibility and experience in return.

They may not be the one pulling you aside to coach you, but if they see you as capable, they'll vouch for you when it matters. And if you listen carefully, they often model the unspoken rules of how to gain credibility in your environment. Use that to your advantage.

THE CREDIT SEEKER

The Credit Seeker is driven by visibility. They want their efforts noticed and aren't shy about claiming them. At their best, they bring energy, initiative, and a sharp eye for opportunity. But their need to be seen can tip into overreach: taking credit for group work, inserting themselves into visible moments, or spotlighting their contributions even when they weren't solo wins.

Strengths:

- Confident in highlighting their value
- Skilled at raising their profile and gaining leadership visibility
- Excellent self-advocate in fast-moving environments
- Frequently seen as ambitious, bold, and high-potential

Weaknesses:

- May take credit for collaborative work
- Struggles to balance self-promotion with shared recognition
- Can alienate teammates by dominating success narratives
- Seen as self-serving when acknowledgment is constant

Self-Reflection: How to know if this is you

You might relate to this persona if:

- You regularly phrase team wins in "I" language
- You insert yourself into projects last-minute to gain visibility
- You feel anxious when your work isn't publicly acknowledged
- You highlight your wins immediately but hesitate to share praise

Real-World Scenario

Your team launches a successful campaign. You've contributed but so did four others. When leadership congratulates the team, you respond with an email that outlines your specific actions and ideas, thanking them for the "opportunity to lead."

The others notice and go quiet. Next time a high-impact project comes up, you're excluded. You got attention, but lost access. The cost of being seen was being trusted.

What to Do Instead:

- Share the spotlight: "It was a great team effort. Sam's data insights made a big difference."
- Build reputation through consistency, not announcements
- Ask for visibility in advance: "I'd love to lead the next conference call. Would that be possible?"
- Let results speak first. Then add your voice with humility.
- Recognition earned through grace earns longer-lasting rewards.

How to Recover

Acknowledge the pattern head-on. Reach out: "I realize I've been overemphasizing my role lately. I want to get better at recognizing everyone's contributions." Then follow up by actually doing it. Start meetings by praising others. Celebrate team wins first. Over time, you'll be trusted again.

How to Navigate This Persona (if it's a colleague)

The Credit Seeker often takes more recognition than deserved, which can be discouraging for new or experienced employees.

How to handle this:

- Document your contributions.
- Speak up in meetings: "Here's what I worked on…"
- Recognize their achievements but protect your own.
- Use tools that track everyone's input.

Focus on consistently delivering clear results to build trust and stay visible.

THE ORACLE

The Oracle has a sharp mind, a quick grasp of detail, and a deep understanding of how things work, especially when it comes to workplace dynamics. They're intelligent, analytical, and rarely wrong. But their downfall? They often act like they have nothing left to learn.

This persona thrives in environments where expertise is valued. However, their tendency to correct others, dominate conversations with facts, or dismiss input that doesn't match their view can become alienating. Over time, coworkers may avoid brainstorming with them. It's not because they aren't smart, but because they leave little room for collaborative growth.

Strengths:

- Highly intelligent and knowledgeable
- Quick to identify flaws or errors
- Strong grasp of systems and structures
- Relied on for technical accuracy or historical context

Weaknesses:

- Can come across as dismissive or arrogant
- Tends to correct rather than collaborate
- Struggles to let others lead or experiment
- Discourages input by dominating or shutting down ideas

Self-Reflection: How to know if this is you

You might relate to this persona if:

- You often interrupt to correct details or "clarify" points
- You assume others don't fully understand things as well as you do
- You grow impatient when people take a different approach
- You mentally rehearse better answers when others speak

Ask yourself: Do I want to contribute or control? What might I learn if I let someone else lead? Do people leave conversations with me feeling smarter or smaller? Wisdom isn't proven by dominating. It's proven by listening, too.

Real-World Scenario

During a planning session, your colleague suggests a solution you've already tried in a previous role. Rather than exploring their reasoning, you cut them off: "That won't work. We tried it before and it failed."

The room goes quiet. The person backs down. The rest of the team becomes hesitant to speak. Later, your manager tells you, "I know you're right most of the time but others aren't feeling heard."

What to Do Instead:

- Ask before correcting: "Can I offer a different angle?"
- Acknowledge before critiquing: "That's a smart take. I'm wondering if…"
- Listen fully before responding
- Let others finish. Even when you think you know the answer

How to Recover

If your feedback style has shut others down, take accountability: "I realize I've been too quick to jump in with answers. I want to make more space for dialogue moving forward." Then act on it. Speak second. Ask more questions. And celebrate ideas that aren't yours.

How to Navigate This Persona (if it's a colleague)

The Oracle can be intimidating and may challenge or correct you. Stay engaged and respond calmly with facts, such as: "That's helpful context. Here's why I'm suggesting this route." Partner with them instead of competing, acknowledge their expertise, and assert your own. Demonstrating competence earns respect and potential support.

CLOSING REFLECTION — THE HUDDLE

Take a breath with me.

You just finished 48 Power Talks on 48 power principles. You learned how to build power circles, grew a strategic network, and now understand how to navigate the 11 personas you'll encounter at work. That's a complete education in workplace power. Most people never get this clarity. You just did.

When we started, I told you this would be like having a coach in your corner. Someone who's been through it and wants to share what actually works. That's what this was. We went through the power principles together, talked about building your circle, identified who to bring close and who to keep at a distance, and mapped out exactly how to handle every type of person you'll face.

This whole book has been about giving you what nobody gave me: a real framework for navigating power as a woman. You're not becoming someone else. You're becoming the most strategic version of yourself. Someone who sees the game clearly and plays it on your own terms.

But here's where it gets real: knowing the principles is valuable. Understanding how to build your network matters. Recognizing the 11 personas helps. But actually using all of this when you're in the middle of it? When that bulldozer is trying to run you over in a meeting? When the manipulator is playing mind games? When you need to activate your power circle to open a door? That's where everything we've worked on comes together.

Think of this book as your comprehensive coaching program: the principles, the relationships, the people dynamics, and the strategy of power. Pair it with my first book, The '48 Laws of Power for Women', which is your playbook. It gives you the specific moves, the exact language, and the step-by-step execution for every power situation.

This was your coaching intensive. That's your field manual. Together, you have everything you need to not just understand power, but to build it, protect it, and wield it effectively.

Because I don't want you to just understand power. I want you to use it.

Here's what you need to know as we wrap up:

Power isn't reserved for the ruthless or the loudest voice in the room. Real power is understanding how the game works and choosing how you want to play it.

It's knowing which power principle applies to your situation right now. It's having a circle of people who will advocate for you when you're not in the room. It's recognizing that the person undermining you is a classic Saboteur and knowing exactly how to handle them. It's understanding that influence isn't built alone. It's built through strategic relationships with people who lift you up.

That's what you've learned here. How to protect your energy and reputation. How to read people and situations before they blindside you. How to build genuine alliances and spot the fake ones. How to adapt your approach based on who you're dealing with. How to stay flexible without compromising yourself.

You now have a complete system for navigating workplace power.

So here's what comes next:

Don't let this knowledge sit unused. This week, pick one power principle and apply it. Reach out to someone in your power circle just to maintain the connection. Notice which persona you're dealing with in your next difficult interaction and adjust your approach accordingly.

Start small. Practice. See how it feels.

Power isn't built in one dramatic moment. It's built through consistent application, daily choices, strategic moves, and relationships you nurture over time. Every time you use what you've learned here, you're strengthening your position. You're becoming someone who moves through your career with intention and clarity.

Picture yourself six months from now:

You're in a meeting and you recognize immediately which personas you're dealing with. You know which power principle applies. You've already activated your power circle to support your position before you even walked in the room. You're not reacting anymore. You're three moves ahead.

That version of you? She's not some fantasy. She's completely achievable. You already have the knowledge. Now you just need to practice.

What We Didn't Get (And Why We Need Each Other)

Here's something I need to say before we close: A lot of what's in this book? Most men learn from their fathers. Not all of them, but enough that it becomes generational knowledge passed down naturally.

They learn how to negotiate. How to speak up in meetings. How to build strategic relationships. How to protect their reputation. How to ask for what they want without apology. These aren't formal lessons, they're observations, casual comments, and advice given over dinner or during a game. "Here's how you handle that situation, son." "Let me tell you what I learned about dealing with difficult people." "This is how you position yourself for the next opportunity."

Many of us didn't get that. Maybe you had a dad who wasn't around. Maybe your father was present but came from a generation where women weren't expected to have careers, so he never thought to teach you these things. Maybe you had a stepfather like mine who believed women belonged at home, so workplace strategy wasn't even on the table. Or maybe your dad meant well but simply didn't know what you'd be up against as a woman in these spaces.

Whatever the reason, there's a gap. And that gap puts us at a disadvantage from day one.

I figured out these lessons the hard way, through mistakes, through watching men move differently than I did, through painful trial and error. That's why I wrote this book. Because if I can spare even one woman the confusion and setbacks I experienced, it's worth it.

But here's the bigger truth: We can't fix this gap alone. We need each other.

I know there's this narrative about women competing with each other, tearing each other down, being threatened by other women's success. And sure, that happens. But it's a trap. It's what keeps us exactly where we are.

Because here's what I've learned: Every single woman, no matter how fast she rises, no matter how talented, no matter how strategic will eventually hit the same ceiling. It might be at different levels, it might look different depending on your industry, but it's there. The structures weren't built for us. The rules weren't written with us in mind.

And when you hit that ceiling, you're going to need other women. Women who understand what you're facing because they're facing it too. Women who will tell you the truth about how they navigated something similar. Women who will advocate for you when you're not in the room. Women who will pull you up because they know that lifting you doesn't diminish them.

This isn't about charity or sisterhood platitudes. This is strategy. When we share information—when we tell each other what actually works, what to watch out for, how to handle the personas we've encountered, we all get stronger. We all move faster. We all get further than we would alone.

Think about it: If your father had taught you these principles at 18, where would you be now? How many mistakes would you have avoided? How much faster would you have advanced?

Now imagine if every woman shared what she learned with the women coming up behind her. Imagine if we treated this knowledge like men do, like something to pass along, not hoard. Imagine if instead of competing for the limited seats we've been given, we focused on building more seats.

That's what I want for us. That's why I'm sharing everything I've learned, even the hard lessons, even the mistakes.

So here's what I'm asking you to do:

Take what you learned here and share it. When you see a younger woman making the same mistakes you made, pull her aside. When another woman asks how you handled a difficult situation, tell her the truth. When you figure out a strategy that works, don't keep it to yourself.

We didn't get the advantage of learning this from our fathers. But we can give each other the advantage of learning from our experiences.

Every time you lift another woman, you're not just helping her. You're strengthening all of us. You're building the network that will catch you when you need it. You're creating the support system that didn't exist for us before.

Because the truth is, we're all playing the same game. We're all facing the same biases, the same double standards, the same invisible barriers. And we can either struggle through it separately, or we can move through it together—faster, smarter, stronger.

I choose together. I hope you do too.

—Mary

About the Author

Mary Robbins writes for women who are tired of performing strength and ready to practice it.

Her work focuses on power dynamics, workplace psychology, and the unspoken rules women are expected to follow and how to break them strategically. Mary's writing blends clarity, humor, and lived experience, offering women language they can use in the moment, not just advice they nod along to and forget.

Her debut book, *The 48 Laws of Power for Women*, became a reader favorite for its sharp reframing of classic power principles through a modern, women-first lens. *Power Talks BullSh*t Walks* continues that work, turning insight into action and conversations into leverage.

If this book resonated with you, Mary would love to hear from you. Leaving a review helps other women find this work and keeps these conversations visible.

Scan the QR code below to explore Mary's other books and resources. If this book supported or inspired you, please leave a review and help empower other women on their journey.

Thank you for reading—and for choosing to speak with intention.

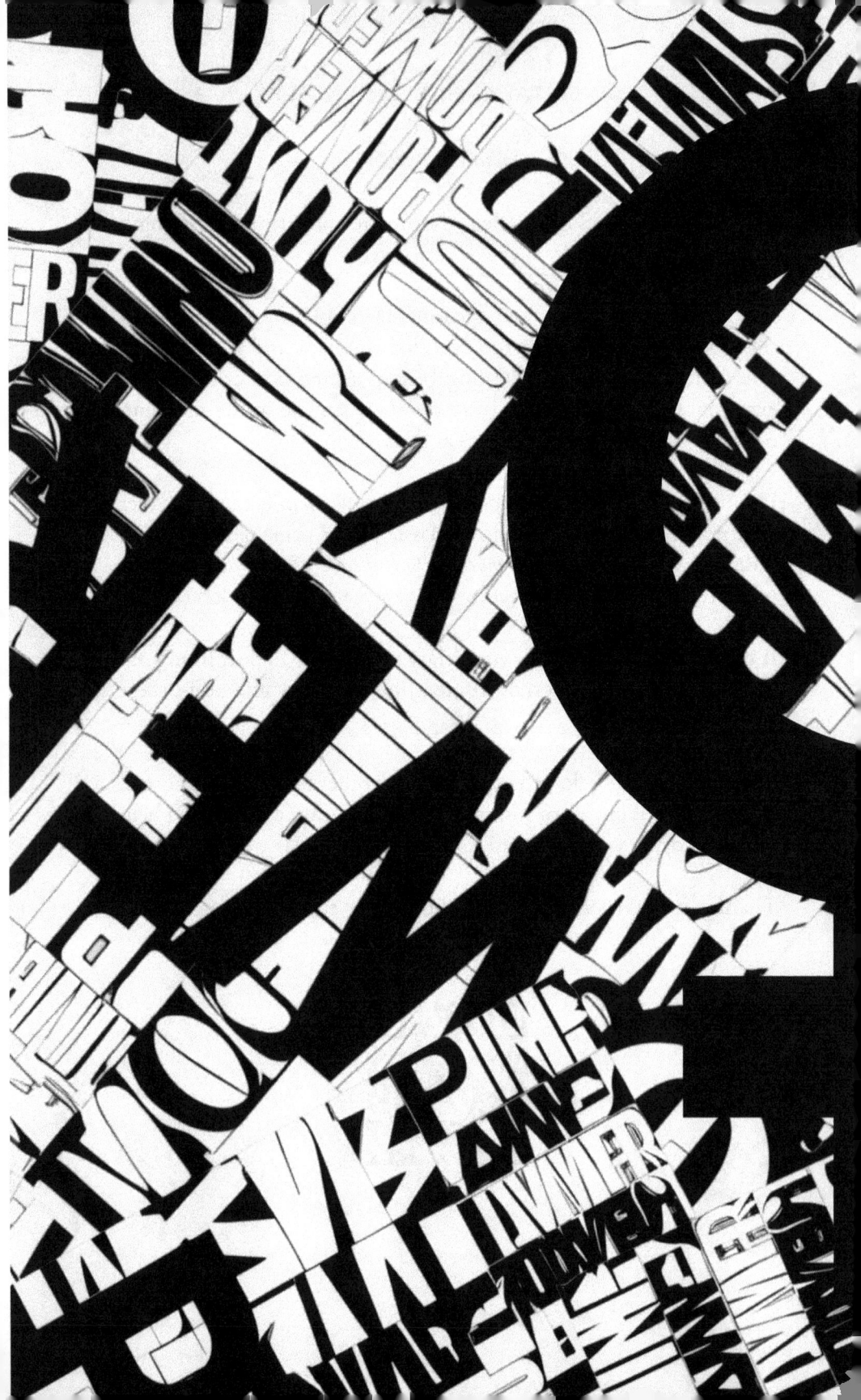

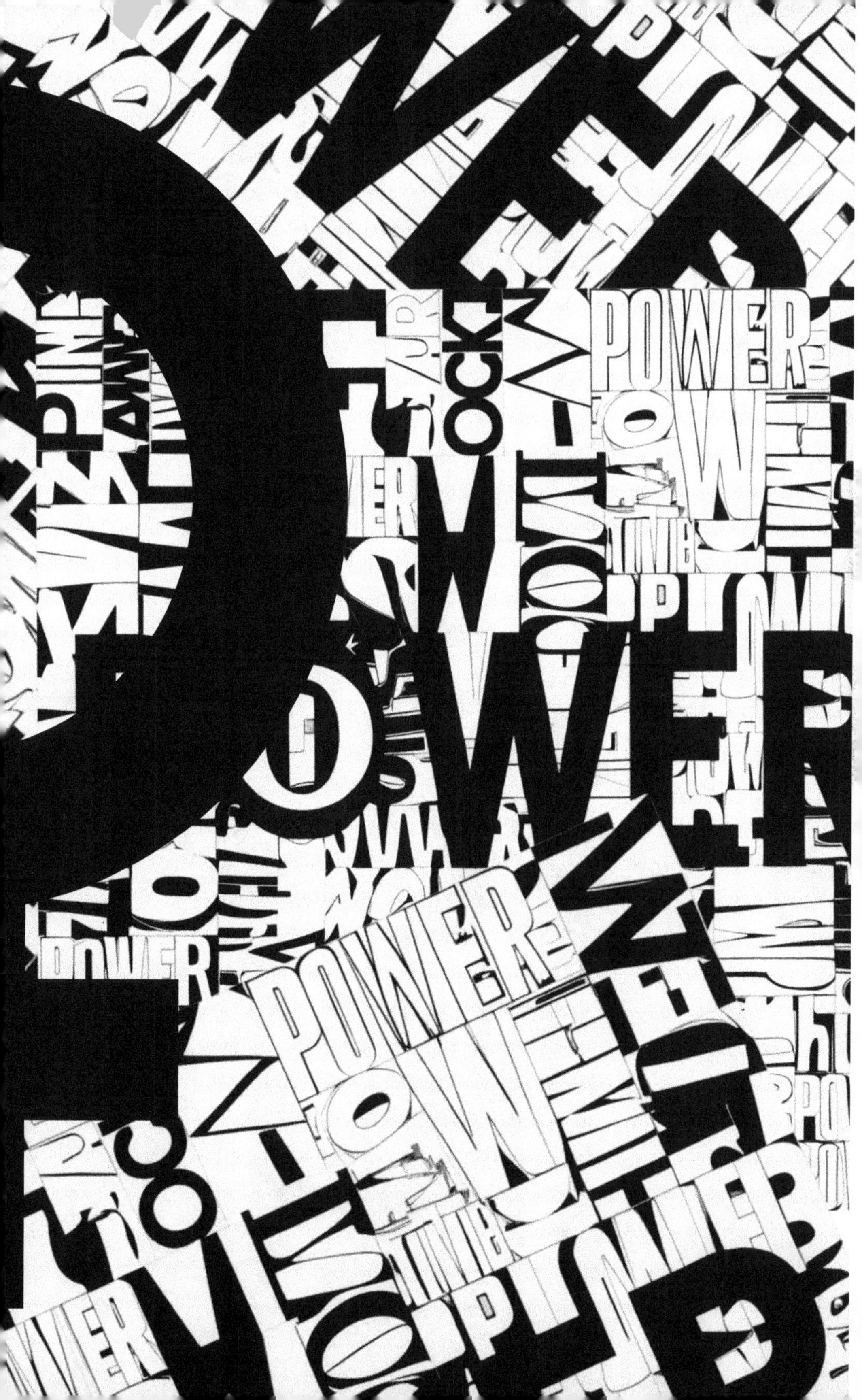
POWER
POWER

www.ingramcontent.com/pod-product-compliance
Lightning Source LLC
Chambersburg PA
CBHW071333210326
41597CB00015B/1437